Tom Sawyer

"A Hymn to Boyhood"
by
Mark Twain

Retold by Henry Brook
Illustrated by Ian McNee

Contents

About
The Adventures of Tom Sawyer

When it was first published in 1876, Mark Twain called his story of Tom Sawyer, *A Hymn to Boyhood*. Twain had set out to write honestly about the fears and thrills of childhood and had turned to his own early life for inspiration. He was already in his forties and had roamed around the world, but Twain remembered every detail of his youth, growing up in a sleepy town on the banks of the Mississippi river. There was a rich store of characters among the friends and river-folk he had known during this time. Twain picked his cast carefully and wove them into a plot as dazzling as any boy's daydream.

According to the author, the book's hero, Tom Sawyer, was "drawn from life" and many of his adventures were based on real events. Twain was always ready to take a risk with his writing style if he thought it would make a story richer and more exciting. Tom doesn't narrate his adventure – as his friend Huckleberry Finn does in a later book – but Twain describes all Tom's thoughts, hopes and worries as he scrambles through a long, hot Missouri summer.

We share Tom's insights and experiences and quickly enter into his world of tricks, challenges and dangerous quests.

Tom Sawyer is a restless scamp, bored at school but blessed with an incredible imagination that helps him outwit his grown-up guardians. He lives comfortably with his adopted family of Aunt Polly, half-brother Sid and cousin Mary, but spends much of his time playing in the woods with an outcast from the town, Huckleberry Finn. Loyal and fearless, Finn is always ready to accompany Tom in his adventures. When the book begins, Tom's chief interests are tricking the local boys, avoiding Aunt Polly's punishments and charming a pretty girl, Becky, who has just started at his school. But the pace of the story suddenly changes when Tom and Huck witness a terrible crime in the town graveyard. The fallout from this scene ripples through the rest of the novel, as Tom and Huck fight for their lives and try to get their hands on a box of buried treasure.

The horror in the graveyard is a sharp reminder of the dangers that prowl on the fringes of Tom's lazy river world. In one section of the book, Tom escapes with two friends to a secret island where they live out their dream of being pirates. Free from school, work and any adult responsibilities, the boys swim, fish and play. But a powerful storm soon disrupts this paradise and rips their campsite to pieces. The risk of violence and sudden death are always lurking beneath the surface of Tom's adventures. This mirrors the unsettled world that Twain had grown up in, with the distant rumblings of change and turmoil always in the background. The state of Missouri supported slavery and Tom's story takes place only a few years before a bloody civil war split the nation and changed the way of life in the slave states forever. After a hopeless stint as a soldier, Twain ran to the Western states to escape the fighting and he never lived in Missouri again.

Twain wrote dozens of books, but the novels describing the lost world of his childhood are among his best. Many readers agree that *The Adventures of Tom Sawyer* features some of his finest writing.

INTRODUCING TOM

The old lady rushed into the room and quickly glanced around. She was hunting for a boy.

"Tom!" she cried.

But there was no answer.

"Tom, where've you got to, you scamp?"

There was still no answer. She pulled her glasses down and peeped over them, then pushed them up and peered under them. She would never look *through* them when she was hunting the hideaway Tom. These were her Sunday-best glasses. She wore them for style, not service, and could see more through a pair of polished bin lids.

"You wait 'till I get hold of you," the old lady snapped. "I'll…"

But she didn't finish her sentence. She was too busy poking under the bed with a broom. All she found was a disgruntled cat.

"You take the biscuit, Tom Sawyer," she sighed.

The old lady stepped over to the open doorway and stared out at the tangle of weeds and tomato plants that made up her back garden. Tom wasn't there. So she filled her lungs with air and boomed: "You-ee, Tom, come here!"

There was a slight noise behind her and she whirled around just in time to catch a small boy by the collar of his jacket.

"I should have known to check that closet," she cried. "What have you been up to in there?"

"Nothing," replied the startled boy.

"But look at your hands," she gasped. "And look at your mouth. What is that mess?"

"I wouldn't know, aunt," Tom gulped.

"I reckon I know," she shrieked. "It's my jam. I've told you forty times to leave my jam alone unless you want a beating. Now pass me that stick."

The whipping stick hovered in the air – Tom was in peril.

"Look at that," he screamed. "Behind you, aunt."

The old lady spun on her heels, snatching her skirts away from the invisible danger. Fast as a bullet, Tom was out of the house and scrambling over the high, garden fence. For a second, his aunt Polly was too dazzled to speak.

Then she broke into a gentle laugh. "That boy outfoxes me every time. I'm just an old fool who can't keep up with all his tricks. He knows how to work my temper up until I want to give him a beating, and then he skips away or makes me laugh and I can't think of raising a hand against him. But I'm not doing my duty, bringing him up like this. Spare the rod and spoil the child, as the Good Book says, and Tom's full of the devil already. But he's my dead sister's boy and I don't have the heart to beat him. It makes me weep when I do, and pains me with guilt when I don't. Well, it's a short life and full of suffering, and I reckon he's just born for trouble. He'll play hookey from school today, I'll bet. So, I'll make him work tomorrow, even though it's Saturday and the other boys will be out playing. I've got to teach him a hard lesson, or I'll be the ruin of that child."

Tom did play hookey that afternoon and he enjoyed every minute of it. He got home just in time for his chores, helping Aunt Polly's slave, Jim, to saw and chop the firewood. In truth, Jim did most of the work, while Tom described his daring adventures. Tom's half-brother, Sidney, had already finished his task of collecting the wood chips. He was a quiet boy and stayed well clear of any trouble – or excitement.

While Tom ate his supper, swiping sugar at every opportunity, Aunt Polly began asking him searching questions. She wanted to lure him into admitting to an afternoon of school-skipping mischief. Like many other simple-hearted souls, she thought she was as crafty as a fox, and mistook her clumsy probing for a marvel of sly cunning.

"Tom," she began, "it must have been warm at school today."

"It was," answered Tom.

"Too hot for books, I'll bet."

"I suppose it was," he replied.

"Didn't you want to go swimming?"

This line of questioning made Tom suspicious. He searched Aunt Polly's face for clues, but it was as blank as a poker player's.

"Not very much," he said cautiously.

The old lady stretched out a hand and touched his shirt cuff. "Is this cloth shirt too warm for you, boy?"

While Aunt Polly flattered herself that she'd checked his shirt for dampness without him knowing, Tom's mind was racing. He'd guessed what she was up to and was plotting how to throw her off the scent.

"Some of us put our heads under the water pump to cool down," he drawled. "Mine's still wet."

Aunt Polly kicked herself for not checking Tom's hair before he'd provided this excuse. She was certain he'd been swimming, and hit upon a new tactic for making him confess.

"You didn't undo your shirt collar, where I sewed it,

Tom, when you went under the water pump? Let me see under your jacket, to check the stitching."

Tom smiled and opened his jacket. His shirt collar was securely sewed.

"You're off the hook, Tom," she told him. "I was certain you'd been naughty and gone swimming, but I misjudged you."

She was sorry that she'd been wrong – and also amazed that Tom had been obedient for once. But then Sidney broke the spell:

"It's funny, Aunt," he said, "but I thought you sewed that collar with white thread."

"That's right, I did," stammered the old lady.

"Well, it's black now," said Sidney, with a smile.

Tom didn't wait for the rest. He was out of the door in a flash, only turning to shout: "I'll get you for that, you traitor."

When he was safely hidden, Tom examined the two needles hidden in his jacket lapel. One was threaded with white cotton, the other with black.

"She'd never have noticed," he hissed, "if it hadn't been for that Sid. But I can never remember if she uses black or white thread. I wish she'd just stick to one and not spoil my schemes. You wait, Sid. I'll teach you a lesson."

Tom was not the local *goody two-shoes*, but he knew the boy who was – and he hated him. But, in less than two minutes, Tom had forgotten all about his despised brother. He had something much more important to occupy his mind: whistling. A man in the town had taught him how to whistle like a bird, flicking his tongue at the back of his mouth to make a liquid warbling sound. It was hard to master, but Tom was soon striding down the street with his mouth full of music and his heart full of thanks to his teacher. He was as happy as an astronomer discovering a new planet. Indeed, when a boy learns to whistle like a bird, he experiences a deeper pleasure than any dusty astronomer at his telescope. He feels in control of all the wild rhythms of the world.

It was summer and the evening sky was still light. Tom suddenly stopped his whistling. A stranger had appeared before him – a boy slightly larger than our hero. Any newcomer in the shabby, riverside village of St. Petersburg was an impressive curiosity, but this boy looked simply astounding. He wore fancy new clothes and a dainty cap, and shoes on his feet – although it wasn't a church day. Tom hated church-best clothes, and loathed any boy who went around dressed up when there was no need for it. The more Tom stared at this overdressed intruder, the more he resented him. Finally, he announced: "I can outfight you,"

"I'd like to see you try it," sneered the stranger.

"Well, I can."

"No, you can't."

"Yes, I can.

"Oh no, you can't."

"Can!"

"Can't!"

There was an uncomfortable pause, and then Tom asked: "What's your name, anyway?"

"That's none of your business."

"I can *make it* my business."

"Let's see you do it."

"If you say another word, I will."

"Word," said the stranger.

"I could beat you with one hand tied behind my back," Tom boasted.

"Then *do* it," cried the other boy.

"I might," replied Tom.

"Well, get on with it. I'm waiting."

"Don't tempt me."

"You're afraid."

"I'm not," snapped Tom.

"Yes you are."

There was another pause, with the boys standing face-to-face, glowering. Tom pressed his shoulder into the stranger's chest, and the stranger pushed back. They struggled until they were both flushed and hot, but neither could get the advantage. Tom stepped back.

"You're a coward and a dog," spat Tom. "I'll tell my big brother and he'll thrash you with one finger."

"I've got a brother too, and he's bigger than yours. He'll throw the two of you over that fence." (Both these brothers were mythical beasts.)

"You're a liar," cried Tom, "and I can still outfight you."

"Prove it," said the stranger.

Tom scratched a line in the dust with his big toe.

"Step over that line," he growled, "and I'll beat you until you can't stand up."

The stranger stepped over the line.

"Are you going to fight me or not?" he smirked.

"I am," said Tom. "For two cents I'd smack you."

The stranger reached into his pocket and took out two small coins. Tom knocked them out of his hand and the next instant the boys were snarling and rolling in the dirt, locked in deadly combat. They tore at each other's noses, hair and clothes, raging in a cloud of dust. Finally, the fog of war cleared and revealed Tom as the champion. He was sitting on the stranger's chest and punching his face.

"Say *give*," shouted Tom.

The stranger mumbled the word of shame and Tom let him up.

"That'll teach you a lesson," said Tom, proudly. "Watch who you fool with next time."

The beaten boy ran off, sobbing, snuffling and shouting threats about what he'd do to Tom the next time they crossed paths. Tom laughed and turned away. As soon as his back was turned, the vanquished boy picked up a stone and hurled it. The missile hit Tom between the shoulders and the stranger ran like an antelope. Tom chased his enemy all the way to his house. He stomped up and down outside the gate, daring him to come out and fight. The stranger stayed indoors, making faces at Tom through a window. At last, the enemy's mother came out and called Tom a bad, vicious and vulgar child. He slunk away, still muttering threats towards the enemy indoors.

Tom got home late, and was ambushed by Aunt Polly as he clambered through his open window. Any doubts she'd been having about punishment quickly vanished when she saw the state of his clothes. Tom would spend his Saturday in captivity, toiling under a hot sun.

THE HAPPY ARTIST

Saturday morning was bright and fresh and brimming with life. There was a smile on every face and a spring in every step. Blossoms perfumed the air and the hills behind the village were lush and green in the morning sun.

Tom Sawyer, his face a portrait of despair, stepped into the road with a bucket of whitewash paint and a long-handled brush. He glanced at Aunt Polly's bare, wooden fence. It was thirty yards long and nine feet high. Tom groaned. Life seemed hollow and his existence just a chore. He sighed and flicked the brush along the first plank, flicked it twice more and then took a step back and compared the one, lonely, whitewashed plank with the hundreds of bare boards stretching away into the distance. Tom sighed and slumped down to the ground.

Jim skipped through the gate, carrying a tin bucket and singing a song. Fetching water from the town pump had always seemed like a trial to Tom, but it didn't strike him that way as he leaned against the fence. There would be friends waiting at the pump, a long line of pals all chatting, playing and skylarking. Tom remembered that Jim always took an hour to get

back with the water, even though the pump was no more than a few houses away.

"Hey, Jim," Tom cried. "Let me take the bucket. You can rest yourself here and do a bit of painting."

Jim shook his head. "I've had special instructions," he said, mysteriously. "The lady of the house told me not to listen to anything you might have to say about whitewashing. She ordered me to keep moving and get down to the pump."

"Never mind what she said," purred Tom. "I'll only be gone a minute and she'll never know about it."

"I don't dare do it, Tom," replied Jim. "She'd give me a beating if she found out."

"She never beats anybody," laughed Tom. "She might give you a telling off, but that doesn't hurt, unless she starts crying. And I've got something for you, if you'll help. I'll give you my prize marble."

Jim hesitated.

"It's the best in my collection," Tom cried.

"That's a pretty marble, no doubt about it," said Jim, admiring the glass orb in Tom's palm. "But I can't risk a beating."

"And I'll even show you my sore toe," said Tom. "It's about ready to drop off."

Jim was too curious to resist this attraction. He put down the bucket and leaned over as Tom unpicked the bandage around his toe. But the next second, Jim was flying down the street with his bucket and a tingling behind and Tom was whitewashing as though his life depended on it. Aunt Polly waved her slipper in the air with a look of triumph.

Tom's show of enthusiasm didn't last long. When Aunt Polly disappeared inside the house, he began to think of all the adventures he was missing. The other boys would be walking past any minute, setting out on amazing quests and expeditions. Tom couldn't bear the thought of them making fun of him for working on a Saturday. He examined his pockets, to see whether he had the means to pay another boy to do his punishment. But all he discovered were bits of toys, marbles and trash. Even bribery was beyond him. Then, at his darkest and most desperate moment, Tom thought of a scheme – a scheme that was nothing less than genius.

He took up the brush and began working. Ben Rogers soon popped around the corner, chomping on an apple and pretending to be a Mississippi paddleboat.

"All hands on deck," he yelled, "turn her about, river pilot, something strange floating up ahead."

Tom didn't blink. He stared at the fence, making sure each brush stroke was perfect.

"Put the paddles in reverse," cried Ben. "What kind of trouble are you in, Tom Sawyer?"

Tom said nothing. He scratched his chin, studied the fence, and lifted his brush like an artist at his easel.

"What's up?" asked Ben, standing next to him. "Why are you working today?"

Tom flicked his head around. "Oh, it's you Ben. I didn't notice you there."

"Yes, it's me," laughed Ben. "And I'm going swimming. Bet you wish you could. Or maybe you'd rather spend your Saturdays working?"

"Who said anything about *working*?" cried Tom. "Do you call this work?" And he turned back to the fence.

"It looks like work to me," said Ben.

"Well it suits me," replied Tom, sharply.

"Don't pull my leg," laughed Ben. "You can't really mean that you *like* whitewashing?"

"Does a boy get the chance to paint a fence every day?" asked Tom, craftily.

That put the whole business in a whole new light for Ben. He stopped nibbling at his apple.

"Can I have a try?" Ben asked.

Tom turned slowly to look at him and shook his head. "No," he muttered. "I just couldn't do it. Aunt Polly is very fussy about this fence. It's got to be a perfect job of painting. I reckon there's only one boy in a thousand, no, one in every *two* thousand, who could do this job the way she wants it."

"Go on, let me try," cried Ben. "I'd let you have a turn, Tom."

"I'd like to, Ben, I would," replied Tom. "But she wouldn't allow it. Jim wanted to try and she wouldn't let him. And Sid was begging for a turn but she turned him down. Can't you see the trouble I'd be in if I was to let you step in, and you messed it all up for me?"

"I'll be careful," pleaded Ben. "I promise I will. And I'll give you the rest of my apple."

Tom looked thoughtful for a minute, then handed over the brush. Ben set to work, sweating in the sun, while the retired artist sat on a barrel in the shade. He dangled his legs and munched on his apple, waiting like a spider for new victims to flutter into his web.

Boys came along to jeer and laugh – and stayed to whitewash. When Ben was exhausted, Tom sold the whitewashing job to Billy Fisher for the price of a kite. Johnny Miller was next in line, after surrendering a dead rat and a length of string to swing it on. Hour after hour, the willing victims came to whitewash. Tom was rolling in wealth by the middle of the afternoon. His pockets bulged with the assorted booty of the village boys: marbles, rusty keys, pieces of chalk, tin soldiers, firecrackers, a brass door knob, a dog collar and four pieces of orange peel.

Tom had discovered one of the great laws of human nature: in order to make a man or boy long for something, all you have to do is make it hard to come by. And, if Tom had been a philosopher and thought carefully about the day's events, he would have understood another human truth. *Work* is everything we are forced to do, and *Play* is everything we choose to do. This truth explains why sleeping under the stars and riding a horse can seem like hard work to a cowboy, but the rich man in a city will hand over his cash to have a chance to do it.

But instead, our hero counted his booty and retreated to headquarters to make his report.

Tom found Aunt Polly in the back room of the house, a space that served as bedroom, breakfast room, dining room and library. She was sitting by an open window and the afternoon's gentle breezes had lulled her to sleep. The family cat was asleep too, curled up in her lap. As Tom came in, the old lady stirred and flicked open one eye.

"Can I go out and play now, aunt?" asked Tom.

"How much have you done?" she coughed, rubbing her face and reaching for the glasses that rested in her hair for safekeeping.

"I've done all of it, aunt. Three coats thick."

"I can't bear it when you lie," replied his aunt, squirming out of her chair.

"It's the truth," protested Tom.

Aunt Polly decided she had to test this claim for herself. She would have been satisfied if Tom had finished one third of the fence. So when she saw that every plank had been lavishly whitewashed, she was astonished.

"Well I never! You can work hard when you put your mind to it," she gasped. But then she added: "Not that you put your mind to it very often. Well, get along and play. Make sure you get back at a reasonable hour, or I'll take my slipper to you. But no, wait one second."

She was so dazzled by Tom's hard work she decided to reward him with an apple.

"A treat tastes all the better when you've earned it through honest effort," she told him, wagging her finger and lifting her eyes heavenwards. Tom saw that she wasn't looking and snatched a doughnut from the jar on the table.

Skipping into the garden, Tom spotted Sid sneaking up the open stairway at the back of the house. The garden was littered with clods of broken earth, and Tom wasted no time launching a barrage against his snake-in-the-grass brother. A hailstorm of clods raged around the traitor, and Tom was over the fence before Aunt Polly could interfere. Sid was left bruised and sobbing, while Tom contented himself that justice had been done.

Our hero knew the pathways around his home better than any alley cat and he was soon safely beyond reach of capture or punishment. He sauntered towards the main square of the village, where two gangs of boys had mustered for a grand battle. Tom was General of one army, and his close friend, Joe Harper, was the military mastermind of the other. These two commanders would not join battle in person. Instead, they sat together, sending messages to their armies through runners. Tom's army won a great victory and the commanders counted their dead, exchanged prisoners and agreed the time and place for their next showdown.

Tom was strolling in the direction of home when he saw a new girl in the garden of Jeff Thatcher's house. Her hair was golden yellow and her eyes were as blue as the morning sky. Our hero gulped and his heart jumped in his chest. He was smitten. But when the blue-eyed angel spotted him swooning on the sidewalk, Tom pretended that he hadn't seen her. Instead, he began showing off with a series of gymnastic leaps and bounds, hoping to impress his new love. Despite his best efforts, he noticed her moving towards the porch of the house, and he rushed towards the fence. Tom heaved a great sigh as the angel placed a perfect foot on the first step of the porch. But his face lit up when she tossed a pansy over the fence, before disappearing into the house.

Tom streaked around to examine the flower, but hesitated before picking it up. He didn't want to appear too eager to seize his lady's *love token*. After dancing around in the street for a moment, he stretched out a foot and scrunched the flower between his toes. Tom hopped away with his treasure and buttoned it inside his jacket, close to his heart. He returned to the fence – and his breathless showing off – but there was no sign of the girl. Tom consoled himself by hoping she had been hiding behind the curtains, watching intently, as he finally trotted home.

Tom was in high spirits all through supper and Aunt Polly wondered if he'd caught a fever. She scolded him for hurling clods at Sid, but Tom couldn't stop smiling. He was so light-hearted, he reached out to steal some sugar from right under his aunt's nose. She rapped him across the knuckles and Tom yelped.

"You don't give Sid a whack when he scoops some sugar," he cried.

"Sid doesn't drive me to distraction the way you do," she replied. "If I didn't keep an eye on you, there'd be no sugar left."

When Aunt Polly stepped into the kitchen, Sid smirked and reached for the sugar bowl. But his smug fingers were too slippery, and the bowl went crashing to the floor. Tom was in ecstasy as the bowl broke and Sid let out a sob. He decided to enjoy every second of Sid's agony, and wait in silence until he was questioned before turning the vandal over for a good beating. Tom could barely contain a whoop of excitement as Aunt Polly came in and began raging over the shattered remains of the bowl. He said to himself: "Now that teacher's pet is going to pay."

The next second, Tom was sprawling on the floor and Aunt Polly was lifting her hand, ready for a second smack.

"What are you belting me for?" Tom shouted. "Sid broke it."

Aunt Polly paused for a moment, but instead of apologizing she only snapped: "Well, I'm sure you deserved it for some other mischief."

Then the old lady's conscience got the better of her, and she yearned to say something kind and loving to our hero. But, she had made a promise to be a strict guardian to the boy, and didn't want to reveal any weakness. Tom sulked in a corner. But secretly he was enjoying himself, fully aware that his aunt was feeling guilty and mean. He ignored her friendly glances, choosing instead to wallow in the self-pity of the wronged man. Tom pictured himself on his deathbed, his health fading away because of the injustice he had suffered over the sugar bowl. His aunt was bending over his body, begging him for one word of forgiveness. But Tom turned his face to the wall in stony silence. Aunt Polly could throw herself at his feet and weep and lament, but Tom would never forgive her.

Tom's feelings were so worked up by this daydream, he began to choke with sadness and a bitter tear trickled the length of his nose. He decided to take himself away from all happy things and places. So when Mary, his cousin, ran laughing into the room, Tom shuffled out through the back door. Mary had been absent for a week, visiting country friends. She wanted to hug and play with her brothers. But Tom was dreaming of misty crags and desolate heaths, sad and gloomy landscapes where he could sink to glorious depths of despair. He dragged his feet to the river and sat down on a log raft.

"If only I could drown myself," he sobbed, "without getting too wet or uncomfortable in the process."

Then he thought of his precious flower. He stared at the poor, wilting pansy and his gloom increased magnificently.

"Would she weep for me," he wondered, "if they dragged me out of the river? Or would she turn away from me like the rest of this cold, heartless world?"

At last, he struggled to his feet and walked home in darkness. On the way, he passed the house of his golden-haired angel and studied every room for a flicker of candlelight. A glow came from an open window on the second floor. Tom climbed the fence and tiptoed across the garden until he was directly below the open window. He lay down on the cold earth, clutching the pansy to his chest. This was how he would die, as a poor, gallant knight pining for his lady. And this was how she would find him: his white fingers gripping her love token and his innocent face staring up at the stars.

A housemaid shouted and a bucket-load of icy water cascaded over the gallant knight. Tom shivered and ran, vaulting the fence as an old boot whizzed past his ear.

Sid woke up to see Tom examining his drenched clothes by candlelight. From the look of danger in Tom's eye, he decided it was best not to ask any questions. Tom went to bed without saying his prayers and Sid made a mental note of his brother's latest sin.

Scholar and Scamp

Sunday was always a difficult day for Tom. On Sundays, the children of the town recited Bible passages at their Sunday school. Sid had a flair for memorizing his verses, but for Tom it was a painful business – like hopping across a field of broken glass. After breakfast, Aunt Polly led the family in worship. Tom fidgeted until his aunt's sermon was over, and then sloped off to begin studying his verses. After thirty minutes of poring over his Bible, he was still in a daze.

"Let me hear you," said Mary, trying to help. "What's the opening line?"

"Blessed are the, *who*?" Tom began.

"The poor," replied Mary, calmly.

"That's right," said Tom, "the poor. But the poor in *what*?"

"In spirit."

"Blessed are the poor in spirit," Tom said confidently, "for they, no wait, it's not *they*, is it?"

"*Theirs*," said Mary.

"Theirs is what?" cried Tom.

"There is the Kingdom of Heaven," said Mary, putting down the book.

"It's too hard," Tom complained. "And besides, I don't want to be a preacher when I grow up."

"It's easy if you try," said Mary. "Look at it again, and I'll give you a present if you get it right."

"That's a deal," said Tom. "But what's the present?"

"I can't tell you that," said Mary, patiently. "But you'll like it, I know you will."

Tom nodded and set to work. With a mystery gift at stake, he became an expert scholar. He recited the verse perfectly and Mary gave him a shiny pocketknife worth more than ten cents. Tom couldn't imagine a finer gift. He was just about to start carving his name on the cupboard door when Aunt Polly ordered him to get dressed and ready for Sunday school.

Before Tom suffered the trial of putting on his Sunday clothes, he faced another ordeal – washing. Mary gave him a basin of water and bar of soap and he paced into the back yard. Tom dipped the soap in the water, put it down on a board and turned up his sleeves. Then he poured the water onto the ground. He came back into the kitchen and wiped his face on a towel hanging on the door.

"Do it again, Tom," cried Mary, pointing outside.

Tom refilled the basin and braced himself for the torture of embracing soapy water. When he staggered into the kitchen, he was dripping with foam. But Mary still insisted on another wash, scrubbing his neck and forehead until he gleamed.

After the wash, came the clothes. Mary buttoned him into a shirt and trousers and crowned him with a straw hat. Tom sulked, and hoped that his sister would forget his shoes. But he was out of luck, and lost his temper as she lifted them out of the cupboard.

"Why do I always have to do things I don't want to do?" he protested.

"Be a good boy," said Mary, smiling.

He got into the shoes, snarling. Then Mary, Sid and Tom set out for Sunday school – something Tom hated with all his heart.

The school ran at the village church, from nine until half-past ten in the morning. A full, holy service followed and, to Tom's disgust, attendance was compulsory. He spied a friend as he was shuffling between the pews.

"Hey, Billy," whispered Tom, "have you got a yellow ticket yet?"

"I have," hissed Billy.

"I want to trade for it," said Tom. "I'll give you a liquorice sweet and a fish-hook."

"Let's see the goods," replied Billy.

The warden of the church had introduced a reward system for his Sunday scholars. When a boy or girl struggled through two recitals, they received a blue ticket. Ten blue tickets earned the child a red one, and ten red tickets could be exchanged for a yellow ticket. Yellow tickets were valuable, and it took months of dedicated Bible studying to win one. But the scholar still had to collect *ten* yellow tickets before he or she hit the jackpot. Gripping these ten yellow coupons, a scholar could march proudly to the front of the church where the warden presented them with a new Bible – worth around forty cents in those days.

Memorizing two thousand verses might seem like a impossible task, but Mary had a pair of them already. Another boy had won four or five of the prizes the previous year, and once recited three thousand verses without stopping. But the pressure of hoarding all those words became too great, and one Sunday his mind snapped around the one thousand mark. He had never recovered and now could barely string a sentence together or remember his own name.

Tom had never hungered for a new Bible. But he longed for the glory – and fame – of winning one. Armed with the treasures from his fence-painting scheme, he began buying tickets from the boys around him. Soon, his pockets were bulging with the coupons.

The warden who supervised Sunday school, Mr. Walters, was sitting on a raised platform at the front of the church. He lifted a hand to silence the frenzied whisperings of Tom and his classmates.

"Sit up straight and concentrate," he commanded. "And don't stare out of the windows. I'm not up in one of the trees, making speeches to the birds. I'm down here, talking to you boys and girls."

He cleared his throat and stroked the white cravat at his throat. It was as crisp as a new banknote.

"I want to tell you how good it makes me feel to see so many bright, clean little faces, who have come here to learn how to be good. And I want to tell you lots of other things."

And he did. But it is not necessary to record his lecture in detail. It's enough to say that it was the same as a million other Sunday school sermons. And, towards the end of it, almost every child in the church was either dozing or whispering with their friends.

As Mr. Walters droned on, the audience of bored children suddenly perked up. A group of adults had entered the church. Mr. Thatcher, the lawyer, was leading a middle-aged couple by the hand. Both man and woman were smartly dressed and had a dignified look about them. The lady was leading a child. Tom almost slipped off his pew when he recognized his blue-eyed angel. He began showing off at once, pinching and cuffing the other boys around him. Any memory of his humiliating drenching under her window was instantly forgotten.

Mr. Thatcher led his guests to a pew at the front of

the church and Mr. Walters introduced them to the congregation. The middle-aged man turned out to be the lawyer's brother. He had climbed to a higher rung of the same profession and was a county judge. The church buzzed with talk and Tom was so impressed by this grand visitor, he almost expected him to let out a mighty roar.

Mr. Walters greeted his guests and proceeded to bore them with a new lecture on village news and other official announcements. He would have given anything to show-off a Bible-winning scholar before the judge, but none of his star pupils had enough tickets. But suddenly, with all hopes for parading a scholar gone, Tom Sawyer stepped forward and demanded a Bible. Walters gasped when he saw the sheaf of tickets gripped tight in Tom's little fist. This was nothing less than a miracle, but the warden had to accept the tickets were genuine. Tom joined the VIPs at the front of the church, beaming with joy as the congregation looked on, stunned. Every boy wanted to trade places with our hero, as he stepped closer to the judge. The noble, legal eagle patted Tom on the head and called him a *fine little man*. Tom was so in awe of the judge – and standing so close to his golden-haired angel – he could barely catch his breath.

"And what is your name?" the judge asked.

"Tom," stammered the boy.

"Is there anything else?" prompted the judge.

"Your full name," hissed the warden. "And don't forget to say *sir*."

"Tom Sawyer, sir," replied our hero.

"So, Tom," said the judge, "you've really recited two thousand verses? That's quite an achievement."

Tom nodded.

"Do not be sorry for the trouble it took to learn them," boomed the judge. "Knowledge is worth more than anything there is in the world. It's what makes a man both great and good. You'll be a great man yourself one day, Thomas, and you'll look back and say thanks to the warden, and thanks for the precious Bible you've earned through all your hard work. You wouldn't trade anything for those tickets, would you? And now, tell my wife and I some of the things you've learned, Thomas? Little boys who study their Bibles should be proud. Why don't you begin with the names of the disciples? Who were the first two to serve our Lord?"

Tom tugged at his collar and blushed. Mr. Walter's heart sank, as he waited for Tom to name Simon and Andrew. Our hero scratched his chin.

"Don't be shy, Thomas," said the judge's wife. "You will tell me, won't you? The names of the first two disciples were..."

"David and Goliath?" Tom blurted, to gasps from the whole assembly.

What happened next is too painful to describe. As a mercy to poor Tom, we will draw a curtain across the rest of that day.

He woke early and groaned into his pillow. Tom had survived his day at Church, but Monday brought a new horror – school. He turned over on his back, thinking that even sickness would be preferable to captivity in the classroom. Wait, perhaps he was sick? It was certainly worth checking. Starting at his toes and working up, Tom examined every inch of his body for bumps, aches and fever. A rumble from his stomach gave him some hopes, but the ripple of muscle pain soon passed. He discovered a wobbly tooth and was about to produce his first, dramatic moan, when he recalled that Aunt Polly was a capable tooth-puller. That would hurt, so he decided to leave the tooth trouble for a back-up scheme.

His only, undeniable injury was his sore toe, but Tom had ignored this possibility for malingering because Aunt Polly had seen him running around on it quite happily for a week or more. But then Tom remembered a story he'd heard about small wounds suddenly festering and striking strong men dead. It was worth a try. Tom groaned with all his might.

Sid let out a snore.

"Wake up, Sid," called Tom. "I'm parting this cruel world."

Sid snored again. So Tom shook him.

"What is it?" cried Sid, pulling at the sheets.

"Don't shake the bed or touch me," moaned Tom. "I'm in mortal pain."

"Tom, what's the matter with you?" Sid shouted.

"I forgive you, Sid," replied Tom, quietly. "I won't hold anything against you when I get to…the other place."

"What are you talking about?" said Sid.

"When I'm gone, give all my treasures to that new girl in town," Tom instructed. "Even my marbles."

But Sid was out of the door and screaming for Aunt Polly. "Tom's dying," he cried. "I've never seen him so bad."

"Rubbish," declared Aunt Polly, climbing the stairs. But her face turned white and her lip trembled when she saw Tom on his deathbed.

"What is it, boy?" she pleaded. "Where does it hurt?"

"It's my sore toe," gasped Tom. "It's gone rotten on me. I believe I'm dying of gangrene, dear Aunt."

Aunt Polly fell across the bed, whooping with laughter.

"Get up and stop fooling around," she told Tom.

"But that's how it feels," argued Tom. "It hurts so much I worried it was dropping off. The pain almost took my mind off my tooth."

"And what, exactly, is wrong with your tooth?"

"It's loose," answered Tom, opening his mouth and pointing.

"So it is," said his Aunt, gripping the tooth with her fingers. "Mary," she cried over her shoulder, "fetch me a silk thread and a lump of hot coal from the fire."

"Don't pull it," screamed Tom, realizing his mistake. "It's fine now. I wasn't really trying to stay at home and miss school."

"So that's what this is all about," Aunt Polly cried. "Tom, I love you so much, but why do you keep trying to break my heart with your naughtiness."

The dental instruments were ready. Before Tom could say another word, Aunt Polly had looped one end of the thread to his wobbly tooth, and the other to the bedpost. She thrust the red-hot coal towards his face and Tom ran. He left the tooth dangling from the bedpost.

Strolling towards school with a fine, black gap in his teeth, Tom met Huckleberry Finn – a boy who struck terror into the hearts of good parents for miles around. Huck was the son of the town drunkard and he was as free as the wind. He was idle, wild and rude and all the boys envied him his freedom. Tom was under strict orders not to play with Huck – so he played with him every chance he got.

Huck dressed in rags and never visited school or church. He would sleep in a doorway in the dry weather, and in a barrel when it rained. Swimming and fishing were his daily occupations, and he was skilled in fighting, smoking and swearing. Huck was a romantic outcast and every boy in the town thought he had it lucky.

"Morning, Huckleberry," Tom called. "What's that you've got?"

"A dead cat," replied Huck, lifting the animal by its tail.

"He's good and stiff," said Tom, admiring the unlucky animal. "What do you want him for?"

"Curing warts."

"How do you do that?"

"You take the cat to a graveyard," Huck began in a whisper. "Go after midnight, and just after someone wicked has been buried. About an hour later, a devil comes to claim the body, but you can't see him. You might just hear a sound like the breeze – that's the sound of the devil's whisper – and when he's taking the body away, you throw the cat after them and shout: Devil follow corpse, cat follow devil, warts follow cat. That's the best cure for warts you'll ever get. Trust me."

"It sounds like a sure-fire fix to me," said Tom. "Have you ever tried it?"

"No," said Huck. "But old Mother Hopkins told me it works."

"She should know," nodded Tom. "People say she's a witch."

"I know she is," replied Huck. "Pap told me. He threw a rock at her one day when he was full of whiskey, and that same night he broke his arm."

"How did he break it?" asked Tom.

"Rolled off a roof he was sleeping on. But it was because that witch put a revenge spell on him, he swears to it."

"Is there any other proof?" asked Tom, fascinated by the story.

"She was mumbling at him when he threw the rock," replied Huck. "It's when they're mumbling that you have to beware. That's when they're saying the Lord's Prayer backwards."

"Hmm," said Tom, staring at the cat. "When are you thinking of trying the cure?"

"Tonight. They buried Hoss Williams the other day."

"Can I come too?"

"If you're not scared."

"Not likely," scoffed Tom. "You make a *meow* under my window and I'll shin down."

"I'll be there," promised Huck. "But don't make me call *meow* too many times before you come. Your auntie's a dead shot with an old boot."

Sweethearts and Swashbucklers

When Tom reached the town's single-room, timber schoolhouse, the rest of his classmates were already busy working at their desks.

"Tom Sawyer!" called the schoolmaster. "Come up here."

Tom approached the master, who was resting in a great wooden armchair at the front of the class.

"You're late, Sawyer, as usual," snapped the master. "What's your excuse today?"

Tom was about to save himself with a well-crafted lie, when he spotted his golden-haired angel sitting on the girls' side of the classroom. The seat next to her was free – and it was the only empty seat on the girls' side of the room. Tom saw his chance and instantly responded: "I've no excuse. I stopped to talk with Huckleberry Finn."

The master's eyes bulged with astonishment and everyone in the room wondered if Tom had lost his mind.

"That's an astounding confession," roared the master. "You've wasted precious school time on that vagrant scamp. Take off your jacket."

Still raging, the master lifted a bundle of sticks from

his desk and whacked Tom across the shoulders five times.

"Now go and sit with the girls," he ordered. "And let that be a warning to you."

The boys tittered but Tom's heart soared. He had guessed how the master would punish him and he hurried over to the angel's pine desk. But she only ignored him and turned to face the window.

Tom waited until the rest of the class was flicking through their books again, and then stole a glance sideways. The girl noticed his peeking and stuck her tongue out at him. She flicked her head around for a full minute, and when she turned back she saw a peach sitting on the desk in front of her. She flicked it away.

Tom gently put it back, and she sent it tumbling. He tried again and this time she allowed it to stay. Tom picked up a piece of chalk and scrawled some words across the slate board on the desk.

"Please take it. I've got more."

The girl read this message, but made no comment. Then Tom began sketching something on the slate, concealing it from her view with the back of his hand. The girl stared straight ahead, but her curiosity soon got the better of her.

"Oh, let me see it," she whispered impatiently.

Tom partly uncovered a scratchy drawing of a house, with four windows, a door, and a corkscrew of smoke rising from its chimney.

"I like it," said the girl. "Do a man."

Tom drew a stick figure as tall as the house and the girl seemed satisfied with the monster.

"Make me come along," whispered the girl.

Tom drew an hourglass with four lines sticking out of it for limbs. The girl sighed.

"That's ever so nice. I wish I could draw."

"I'll teach you," offered Tom.

"When?"

"At noon, if you like. Do you go home for lunch?"

"I'll stay if you will," replied the girl.

"It's a date," said Tom, beaming. "What's your name?"

"Becky Thatcher. And you're Tom Sawyer."

"That's what they call me when they're getting ready to whack me for something. Call me Tom."

He began sketching some words over his drawing,

again hiding his work from the girl. But she begged him to let her see.

"It's nothing," said Tom.

"Yes it is," she answered, flashing her eyes.

"You don't want to see it."

"Of course I do."

"Will you keep it secret?"

"I won't tell a soul."

"Oh," he teased, "I can't trust you. And you might not like it."

Becky put her small hand on Tom's and struggled with him over the slate. Tom let her drag his fingers away, revealing the words: I LOVE YOU.

"You bad boy," she whispered, and slapped his hand. But Tom saw that she was blushing and thought she looked pleased by her discovery.

The next instant, Tom's ear was burning hot. The master was towering above him, pinching and lifting our Romeo out of his seat. He dragged Tom across to his old seat with the boys. The whole class was giggling.

Tom tried to study, but he was yearning to be reunited with the angel and found it impossible to concentrate on his reading, his geography, and his spelling. Books seemed dull and stifling, and the minutes dragged like hours as he waited for noon break. At last, the master released his students and Tom flew to Becky's side.

"Pretend that you're walking home," he whispered in her ear, "and then double back and meet me here, alone."

After slipping away from their friends, the knight and his lady sat down together at one of the desks in the deserted schoolroom. Tom placed a slate across his lap and held Becky's hand as she sketched out a leaning, wobbly-walled house. When they lost interest in art, they chatted.

"Do you like rats?" asked Tom, thinking of the rodent he had collected on Saturday.

"Oh no," cried Becky. "I hate them."

"Even dead ones?" asked Tom.

She nodded. "What *I* like," she told him, "is chewing gum."

"I wish I had a bit to give you."

"I've got some," she said, smiling. "You can have a chew, but I want it back."

They sat, sharing the gum. Tom had never been happier.

"Have you ever seen a circus?" he asked.

"Of course," she nodded. "And my Pa's promised to take me again, if I'm good."

"I love the circus," declared Tom. "I'm going to be a circus clown, when I grow up."

"Oh, that's nice. I love their costumes," said Becky.

"They make a dollar a day," replied Tom. "And Becky, have you ever been engaged?"

"Engaged with what?" she asked.

"I mean, engaged and getting ready to be married," he explained.

"No."

"Would you like to?"

"What's involved?"

"It's simple," said Tom. "You tell a boy you won't care for anyone else but him, or marry anyone else, ever, and then you kiss."

"What's the kiss for?"

"People always do that when they get engaged."

"Everybody?" she asked.

"Everybody that loves someone. Do you remember what I wrote on the slate?"

"I suppose."

"What was it?"

"I don't want to say."

"Shall I tell you again?" asked Tom, with his best puppy dog eyes.

"Some other time," replied Becky, coolly.

"I have to do it now," begged Tom. "I'll whisper it in your ear."

Becky hesitated but Tom slipped an arm around her waist and whispered the words into her golden hair.

"Now you whisper it to me," he told her.

But she resisted. "Turn your face away so you can't see," she demanded. "And you won't ever tell, will you, Tom?"

"Not a soul," replied Tom.

She whispered the words into his curly hair and then she was up with a bound and running between the desks. Tom chased after her, and finally cornered her next to the blackboard. Becky held her white apron up over her face like a mask.

"You forgot the kiss," he cried.

"I didn't forget it," she answered. "That's why I ran."

But she soon surrendered to her pursuer's pleadings, dropping her apron and lifting her face. Tom kissed her red lips.

"It's all done, Becky," he laughed. "You can't love or marry anyone but me now, do you understand? We're bound together for eternity. And even longer than that."

"I'll never love anybody but you, Tom," she cried. "I like being engaged so much. And I'd never even heard of it before."

"It's easy when you've done it once or twice," replied Tom, casually.

Becky wailed and began to cry. "You mean you've done this before?"

"But I don't love any of those girls any more," stammered Tom.

All was lost. Becky pressed her face to the blackboard and wept.

"I don't care about anyone except you," Tom howled. "I swear it, Becky."

She answered him with sobs. Nothing he could say seemed to help. He offered her his best treasures, but she pushed them away. Feeling helpless – and rejected – Tom's despair turned to anger. If she couldn't forgive him, he would take himself off into exile. He stormed out of the school and ran towards the distant hills.

Tom climbed out of the town, following a track that led past Widow Douglas' house. The widow had been married to a wealthy judge, and her mansion was the grandest building in St. Petersburg. It stood alone in acres of woodland and Tom darted between the trees, wandering deep into the wilderness. He had a secret den in the woods, and when he reached the spot he sat down on a mossy stone under the canopy of an ancient oak tree. It was so quiet, not even the birds were singing. Tom rested his chin in his hands and thought things over. It didn't take long for him to decide that life was nothing but trouble.

"Sometimes I think I'd rather be dead," he muttered to himself. It would almost be worth drowning himself in the river, to see Becky sobbing at the graveside. If only he could die *temporarily*, Tom pondered. He didn't want to miss all the weeping and wailing over his poor, dead body.

Perhaps, if he ran away, Tom wondered, people might think he was dead? He could travel to unexplored countries across the seas, and disappear for years. There was no room for happiness in his life, so he abandoned the idea of being a clown in the circus. He would be a flint-faced soldier, and return to the town in his bloody uniform, weighed down with medals. Better still, he could join a tribe of Native Americans – the Sioux or the Apache. He was an outcast from polite society, after all. Tom imagined himself hunting for buffalo and clambering over great, snowy mountains where even eagles were scared to fly.

"They'll make me a chief," he chuckled. Tom would storm into the Sunday school one sleepy, summer morning, dripping with war paint and waving a razor-sharp tomahawk over the warden's scalp.

But soldiers and Sioux warriors were too tame for Tom's taste, he decided. He wanted to do something shocking – something *bloodcurdling*. Tom would be a pirate. That was the answer, he realized suddenly, jumping up in excitement. People would shudder when they heard his name: *Black Tom*, scourge of the Spanish Main. At the height of his fame, he would kick down St. Petersburg's church doors. Weather-beaten, swarthy and scarred, our hero would stride to the front of the hall.

"It's Black Tom," people would scream. "Back after all these years, for vengeance on his betrayer, Becky Thatcher. Run for your lives."

He would leave for the ocean in the morning.

With the problem of his future career settled, Tom got back to the important business of enjoying himself. He was deciding what to do for his next adventure, when he heard the blast of a toy trumpet, ringing through the forest. Tom dropped to his knees and began rummaging in some bushes around the oak tree. He uncovered a stash of treasures: a small bow and arrow, a wooden sword and a tin trumpet. Quickly, Tom armed himself with the weapons and blew a rasping note through the trumpet. This brought a return signal from the other cornet player, and Tom went racing through the woods towards the sound.

He burst into a clearing among the trees and lifted his sword. "Where are you, my merry men?" Tom cried.

Joe Harper stepped into the clearing, armed like Tom with a sword and bow.

"Who is this varlet," asked Tom, "who enters Sherwood Forest without my permission?"

"Guy of Gisbourne," replied Joe, boldly. "And he goes where he pleases. Who is this weasel that challenges Guy?"

"I am Robin Hood," declared Tom, sticking his chest out and lifting his chin. "And your sword-sliced carcass shall soon know it, verily, indeed yes."

"Right gladly will I dispute with thee the lordship of this merry wood," said Joe, with a gasp. "To swords."

The two boys raised their swords and began to slash and jab at each other. Soon, they were sweating and panting from the work.

"Fall! Why don't you fall?" cried Tom.

"It's your turn to fall," snapped Joe.

"That's not what the book says," Tom replied. "You have to turn around and let me slay you with one stroke."

Joe bowed to the authority of the book and received the whack without complaint.

"Now," he barked, jumping up and brandishing his sword. "You have to let me kill you. It's only fair."

"But you can't kill Robin," shouted Tom. "It goes against the story."

"Why is it you that always gets to do the killing?" cried Joe. "I want a turn."

"You can be Robin for a while," Tom suggested. "I'll be the Sheriff of Nottingham, and you can kill him any day of the week."

Joe was satisfied. He hacked away at the Sheriff until he delivered a death stroke, and Tom sank to the ground, moaning. Tom died and changed shape again, turning into a band of outlaws storming Robin's forest lair. The battle raged until the light began to fade. The two outlaws hid their weapons and picked their way out of the woods, moving towards the glimmering lights of the town.

In the Graveyard

Tom and Sid were sent to bed at half past nine, as usual. Sid was soon asleep but Tom lay awake, counting the seconds in restless impatience. He stared into the dark, listening to the night sounds and longing for midnight. When the clock struck ten, Tom's heart sank with despair. Every minute passed in agony, until his mind began to drift and dream and he slipped into sleep.

Tom didn't hear the eleven o'clock chimes. But, a little later, he shuddered at the sound of a window scraping open. A strange, wailing sob mingled with his dreams and a shout woke him: "Scat, you furry pest." In less than a minute, Tom was dressed and crawling across the roof to the rear of the house. Huckleberry Finn was crouching, waiting for him in the back yard, armed with his dead cat.

It took them thirty minutes to walk out to the graveyard, which was perched on a hill a mile from the town. There was a sagging plank fence guarding the perimeter and waist-high grass and weeds grew wild everywhere, curling around the wooden grave markers. A low breeze whistled and moaned through the trees, and Tom feared it might be the voices of dead spirits and ghouls warning him to leave. He spoke only in whispers with Huck, while they hunted for the new grave. At last, they found a freshly turned pile of earth and hid themselves behind some old elm trees a few feet away.

They waited in silence for the devils to come. But only the hooting of an owl broke the stillness.

"It's awful quiet," whispered Tom. "Do you think the dead people like us being here?"

"I wish I knew," said Huck.

"Do you think Hoss Williams hears us talking?"

"I reckon his spirit does."

"I wish I'd called him *Mister* Williams just then," said Tom, sadly. "But everybody calls him *Hoss*."

"That's what thery *used* to call him," whispered Huck. "But I reckon he's not too particular about it now."

Tom heard a scraping sound, rising on the breeze.

"Did you hear that, Hucky?" he asked.

"I've got ears. I heard it."

"They're coming," hissed Tom, trying to stop his voice from trembling. "What should we do?"

"If we keep still, they might not see us," whispered Huck.

"I bet they can see in the dark, like cats. I wish I'd never come."

"Don't be scared," said Huck, softly. "We're not doing them any harm, are we? Try to keep still, and they won't notice us behind this tree."

"I'm trying," Tom replied. "But I've got the shivers."

"Look!" said Huck, peeking over a branch. "Do you see that?"

"What is it?" gasped Tom.
"Devil fire. And it's coming this way."

Some figures approached through the gloom, swinging a lantern that cast terrible shadows over the graves.

"Three devils," whispered Huck. "Tom, we're goners. Do you know any prayers?"

"I can't remember any," sobbed Tom, suddenly remembering the safe haven of Sunday school.

"Wait! It's all right, Tom, they're human. I think I hear that old drunkard Muff Potter's voice."

Tom strained his ears and heard broken words coming from the trio of devils. "You're right, Huck," he whispered. "And I reckon I know one of the others. It's Injun Joe."

Huck gasped and was about to reply, but thought better of it. The three figures had reached the new grave and were only yards from the boys' hiding place.

"Here it is," said a gruff voice. The man lifted the lantern to his face and Tom recognized the town surgeon, Dr. Robinson.

Potter and Injun Joe grunted and threw their hats down in the grass. They took two shovels from a cart they were dragging and dug into the grave. The doctor fixed the lantern on a board and sat down with his back to one of the elm trees. He was so close to the boys, Tom could have reached out and touched his shoulder.

"Hurry it up," the man ordered. "The moon might be out any minute."

The diggers growled and worked harder. Tom soon heard a shovel strike something hard and watched as the men dragged a coffin into the open. One of the grave robbers forced its lid off with the tip of his shovel. He dragged the body out and dumped it in the grass. Suddenly, a bright moon slid from behind the clouds and Tom stared in horror at the bloodless face of the dead man. Potter went off to rummage in the cart and returned with a blanket and some rope. He wrapped and tied the corpse and lifted it onto the cart.

"Now he's ready for you, Doc," snarled Potter, cutting the rope with a hunting knife. "But he's going back into the ground if we don't see another five dollars from you."

"Well said," coughed Injun Joe.

"I don't understand," cried the doctor, getting to his feet. "You asked for payment in advance, and I've paid you *in full*."

"Well, we want some more," said Injun Joe. "And you're getting off lightly, when I think what you did to me five years ago."

"I-I-I don't know what you're talking about," stammered the doctor.

"Have you forgotten that night when I came to your house?" hissed Injun Joe. "It was five years ago, and I was hungry, asking around for a scrap of food. You turned me away. And when I cursed you, and said I'd get even with you one day, your father had me jailed for vagrancy. Well, this is my revenge. So hand over the money."

Injun Joe raised his fists, but in a flash the doctor punched him to the ground.

"Don't you hit my buddy," shouted Potter, and he dropped his knife and charged at the doctor. The two men grappled with each other, stamping in the dirt with their boot heels. While they struggled, Injun Joe pulled himself up and searched in the grass for Potter's knife. The doctor suddenly broke free, snatched up the board by Williams' grave and used it to knock Potter out cold. He crumpled to the ground. At the same instant, Injun Joe rushed in and sank the knife into the young man's chest. The doctor tottered and fell across Potter, splattering him with blood. Tom thought he might scream, but the moon suddenly vanished into the clouds and he and Huck crept away in the darkness.

Injun Joe stood over the two men by the grave, weighing up the situation. The doctor murmured a few, strangled words, gave a long gasp and was still.

"That's settled my score with you," spat Injun Joe.

He robbed the dead doctor's body. After this, he worked Potter's knife loose and pressed it into his old friend's palm. A few minutes passed and then Potter began to stir. His hand closed on the knife. He lifted it, glanced at the doctor's body and dropped the weapon in the grass.

"I'm frightened," he cried, looking into Injun Joe's eyes. "What's happened here?"

"It's a dirty business," Joe replied. "Why did you do it?"

"I've done nothing," squealed Potter.

"This doesn't look like nothing," said Joe, nudging the doctor's body with his boot.

"It's the whiskey," cried Potter. "I shouldn't have taken a drink tonight, I must have gone crazy."

"That's how it looked."

"But I don't remember any of it," said Potter. "Tell me, Joe, be honest with me. Did I really do it? Did I murder the young doctor?"

"You were fighting," answered Joe, "and then he knocked you over with the headboard. You jumped up and screamed like a wild man. Before I could stop you, you'd grabbed the knife and stabbed him. He landed another punch on your chin as he was falling. You've been lying there as still as a dead man for the last ten minutes."

"I didn't know what I was doing," said Potter. "I was in the whiskey haze, I must have been. I've never killed a soul before, Joe. I'm not a violent man. But you won't tell, will you, Joe? You're my buddy. And I've always backed *you* up when you were in trouble."

"You've been fair and square with me, Muff Potter," answered Injun Joe. "I won't turn you in."

"Oh Joe, you're a friend for life," Potter blurted.

"Don't cry like a baby," snapped Injun Joe in disgust. "Get moving down the hill and try not to leave any tracks. I'll head off the other way."

Potter loped off into the dark and Injun Joe stood looking after him. He glanced down to where the knife still lay in the grass, and smiled. A moment later, he had vanished into the night.

A Painful Secret

The two boys raced towards town, speechless with horror. They looked over their shoulders from time to time as they ran, checking to see that there was nobody chasing after them.

"Let's get to the old tannery on the edge of town," whispered Tom. "My lungs are almost bursting and we need somewhere to hide."

Huck nodded and pushed his legs to work even harder. Shoulder to shoulder, the boys burst through the open doorway of the tannery shed and fell in a heap among the shadows.

"What a terrible sight," Tom coughed, trying to catch his breath. "What's going to come of this, Huck?"

"A hanging, I reckon," replied Huck. "What else?"

"But who's going to say what happened?" asked Tom. "Are we?"

"What are you suggesting?" gasped Huck. "Do you want to take the risk of turning in Injun Joe? What if he *doesn't* hang, and he finds out about us being there? He'd murder us both as sure as my name's Huck Finn. Let Muff Potter do the talking."

"But Potter didn't see it," said Tom. "He was out

cold. He might even be dead, for all we know."

"I doubt it, Tom," sighed Huck. "He'd been drinking, I could tell from his voice. When Pap's full of whiskey, you could hit him over the head with a church and it would only give him a headache. Muff Potter might be a bit dazed, but I don't think he's dead."

"But could you really keep mum about what we saw?" asked Tom.

"I don't think we've got any other choice," answered Huck. "Injun Joe would drown us like a pair of cats if he knew what we'd seen. We've got to swear to each other that we'll never say a word about it."

"I'm with you, Huck," cried Tom. "If we speak out we're dead men. Let's swear and shake hands on it."

"That won't do," replied Huck, in a solemn voice. "This is a serious business and it needs to be signed and sealed properly. There ought to be writing, to make it official, and some blood spilled."

Tom nodded. The idea of making a blood oath, long after midnight, appealed to his love of pirates, outlaws and other desperadoes. He picked up an old, wooden roof tile that lay in the moonlight and scrawled some words across it with a piece of chalk from his pocket:

HUCK FINN AND TOM SAWYER SWEAR TO KEEP MUM AND WISH THEY MAY DROP DOWN DEAD IN THEIR TRACKS IF THEY EVER TELL AND ROT.

Tom read out the oath, and Huck complimented his friend on his fine use of language. The boys pricked their thumbs with one of Tom's lapel needles, and signed their initials to the oath in a trickle of blood. Finally, they buried the tile by the tannery wall.

"Silence, or death," whispered Tom.

Huck repeated the words and the two friends shook hands and hurried off on their separate ways.

It was almost dawn when Tom climbed through his bedroom window. Sid was snoring, so Tom carefully undressed and slipped into bed beside his brother. He never guessed that Sid was secretly awake, and had been for more than an hour.

When Tom opened his eyes, Sid was gone. The sun was high in the sky, and Tom was startled that nobody had been up to call him for breakfast. He tumbled downstairs feeling stiff and sleepy. The family was still at the breakfast table, but they had finished eating. Tom expected a scolding but Aunt Polly turned her eyes away from him and said nothing. The silence was worse than a thousand floggings, thought Tom, and he was relieved when she finally asked him to join her at the front of the house.

"My heart's broken with your wicked ways," she told him, quietly. "It's no use me trying to help you any longer," she went on, as the tears welled up in her eyes. "I've given up on you, Tom. Everything I try makes no difference. You've turned my hair white with worry and I see no possible way to save you."

Tom's heart ached more than his sore and sleepy body. He cried and pleaded for his aunt's forgiveness, promising that he would be good. At last, Aunt Polly stopped weeping and sent him away. Tom left the room feeling miserable and alone. He had no hunger for revenge against the traitor, Sid, and tramped off to school, staring gloomily at the dust under his feet.

The master flogged Tom and Joe Harper for playing hookey the day before, but Tom barely noticed the pain. Becky wouldn't look at him. He shuffled to his seat with the numbed and hopeless expression of a man who has suffered long years of lonely captivity. It was hard to imagine how things could be worse.

At noon, the whole town was electrified by news of bodysnatching and murder. The word passed between the houses like a thunderbolt and nobody blinked an eye when the schoolmaster announced that class was suspended for the rest of the day.

As the townsfolk drifted towards the graveyard, Tom's heartbreak vanished and he joined a curious mob on the road. A man was telling what he knew of the grim story and how a bloody knife had been discovered next to the doctor's mutilated body.

"I heard a whisper that it was Muff Potter's knife," reported the man.

There were gasps and sighs from the crowd.

"And Potter was seen, washing himself in a stream around two in the morning," added the man.

"Him, washing?" cried a woman, as though this was evidence enough that Potter was the killer.

"The Sheriff can't find him anywhere," said the man. "But riders are out, searching the vicinity."

Tom pushed his way through the crowd around the graveyard. Even though his heart raced with terror at the thought of returning there, Tom was driven on by a dreadful fascination. He wormed his way through a ring of gawpers and found himself staring straight into the doctor's glassy eyes.

Somebody pinched his arm and Tom spun around to see Huckleberry. But the two boys looked away from each other, not wanting to draw attention to their awful secret.

"Muff Potter will hang for this," cried one of the spectators at the graveside.

"If they catch him," replied another.

Tom shivered from head to heel when he caught sight of Injun Joe's sallow face, peering at him through the crowd. But there was a shout and the killer turned his head with all the others.

"He's here, I can see him coming," called a voice.

"Who's here?" shrieked a woman.

"Potter," replied a boy, who had climbed one of the elm trees to get a better view. "But he's stopped. I think he's trying to get away."

Tom craned his head over a man's shoulders and saw Potter, confused and frightened, standing on the other side of the graveyard.

"Revisiting the scene of the crime, I'll bet," said a man next to Tom.

The crowd parted to let the Sheriff step through. He took Potter by the arm and led him over to the corpse.

When he stood before the murdered man, Potter's face turned white and his whole body trembled. He put his face in his hands and burst into tears.

"I didn't do it, friends," he sobbed. "I didn't kill him."

"Who said you did?" shouted a voice.

Potter looked up, shaking with fright. He spotted Injun Joe trying to hide himself in the throng, and called to him: "But Joe, you promised you wouldn't."

"Is this your knife?" the Sheriff demanded, thrusting the knife under Potter's nose.

Potter's knees gave way when he saw the blood-smeared blade. He would have fallen if the Sheriff and his deputy hadn't caught him by the arms.

"I knew I should have come back for it," he said, weakly. "But I was too scared to do it in the dark. Well, there's no hope for me now. Tell them, Joe, tell them everything that happened."

Huck and Tom stood with their mouths open and their eyes staring wild, while the killer calmly described how Potter had stabbed the doctor.

"He's signed a deal with the devil," whispered Huck at Tom's ear. "No ordinary man could lie like that."

When Injun Joe finished his story, the Sheriff dragged Potter away. Injun Joe helped to lift the doctor's body into a cart and then melted back into the crowd. Still shocked by what they had heard, Tom and Huck joined the gloomy procession of townsfolk behind the cart as it creaked and swayed away from the graveyard.

Over the following days, Tom's secret gnawed away at him, disturbing his sleep. At breakfast one morning, Sid complained that Tom was tossing and turning so much it was keeping him awake.

"It's a bad sign," said Aunt Polly, gravely. "What's on your mind, Tom?"

"Nothing," Tom lied, and his hand trembled so much that he spilled his coffee.

"And that's only part of it," Sid added. "He keeps talking about *blood*, and how he can't stand being tormented any longer and he must tell somebody. What is it you have to tell, Tom?"

"It's that dreadful murder," Aunt Polly said, interrupting. "I keep dreaming about it myself and having crazy thoughts about who did it. Leave your poor brother alone, Sid."

Sid seemed satisfied with this explanation. That evening, Tom said his teeth were aching and he wrapped a bandage around his jaws. He didn't want any more words to slip out, while he dozed. The sly Sid waited until Tom was snoring and then worked the bandage free, hoping to learn his brother's secrets. But if he made any sense of Tom's ramblings, he kept it to himself.

Every day or two, Tom made the furtive journey out to the town prison; a brick hut on the edge of the town. There were no guards to watch over Potter, and Tom passed the prisoner bits of food through his barred window. Potter was grateful for any kindness, and the good deeds helped to ease Tom's guilty conscience.

There was heated discussion among the townsfolk that week, concerning Injun Joe. The great majority of them wanted to tar and feather the villain for his part in the bodysnatching. But everyone was so scared of the man, nobody came forward to do the job. Injun Joe's statement to the Sheriff described the murder, but he had been careful not to mention the grave robbing beforehand. The Sheriff warned him to stay close to town, so he could be a witness at Potter's trial. Until then, Injun Joe was free to come and go as he pleased.

THREE PIRATES

Tom's spirits finally lifted two weeks after the killing, when Becky Thatcher returned to school. His angel had fallen ill the day after the murder, and her long absence had only added to Tom's misery. Watching Becky arranging books and pens across her desk, Tom resolved to win her back with a breathtaking display of gymnastics and daring horseplay. At morning break, Tom shouted and whooped, chased the other boys and vaulted the school fence.

But when he stole a glance over to Becky, Tom saw that she had turned her back on his performance. He ran towards her, snatching a boy's cap from his head and hurling it onto the roof of the schoolhouse. Becky didn't blink. In desperation, Tom broke through a group of students standing close to his sweetheart, tumbling boys in every direction and landing in a dusty heap, right at her feet. Becky turned her nose up at him.

"Some people think they're so smart," she snapped. "But no amount of showing off is going to impress me."

Becky crossed her arms and marched away, leaving her admirer crushed and crestfallen in the dirt.

With all his hopes for a renewed engagement with Becky dashed, Tom stumbled away from school feeling alone and unloved. There was nothing left for him here in St. Petersburg, he told himself. He let out a sob and began to cry. The world was too cold and cruel and it was time to go to sea.

Rubbing his eyes to clear the tears, Tom noticed his friend Joe Harper approaching on the road.

"Joe," he called, "you see before you a broken man. I've been treated harshly and have decided to leave this place, cross the seas and vanish forever. Do not forget me, my old friend. I'll try to write."

Joe blurted out that he had come looking for Tom to deliver the same, gloomy message.

"I've been whipped, unjustly, Tom," he raged. "My mother beat me for stealing some cream, even though

I knew nothing about it. It's the final straw, Tom. She cares nothing about me, so, I've decided to run away and find a cave somewhere, to live like a hermit until I die of starvation and loneliness."

Tom soon persuaded his friend that pirates had more adventures than hermits. They would join forces, find a ship and steal some treasure.

"We'll make a start on the Mississippi River," said Tom. "There should be rich pickings for desperadoes like us. But first, we'll need a base."

The boys decided that Jackson's Island would be ideal for their headquarters. This long, wooded island in the Mississippi was only three miles below St. Petersburg. Nobody lived there, and it lay close to the wild, far shore, so they would be safe from any prying eyes. Tom and Joe invited Huck Finn to join their pirate band and he accepted, eagerly. The three friends agreed to meet again at midnight, to steal a log raft from one of the rafters' camps upriver.

Tom arrived at the meeting place carrying a leg of boiled ham and a bag of clothes. There was a bright moon in the sky and the mighty river rolled by like an ocean at rest. Tom whistled softly and heard the return signal from his two friends.

"Who goes there?" growled a voice.

"Black Tom. Name your names."

"Huck Finn the Red-Handed and Joe Harper, the Terror of the Seas."

"Give the password," hissed Tom, and all three boys shouted together: "BLOOD."

They hurried to the riverbank and soon found a small raft roped to a tree stump. All the rafters were in town, buying supplies or drinking liquor, and the boys quickly loaded their belongings onboard and shoved off from the shore. Tom gave his orders in a stern whisper.

"Bring her into the wind, Terror of the Seas."

"Aye, aye, sir," answered Joe, in a growl.

Joe and Huck poled the raft into the middle of the river and a gentle current carried them downstream. A few lights from St. Petersburg shimmered across the water and Tom thought of his sleeping friends and family, all unaware of his great adventure. Black Tom crossed his arms and wished Becky could see him sliding by on his pirate ship, floating off to certain doom with a grim-faced smile.

They landed on the sandy banks of Jackson's Island and waded back and forth with their food and other possessions. Huck discovered an old piece of sail snagged among the trees by the shore and the boys used it to make a tent for their belongings. The pirates would lie down to sleep under open skies, as is the custom of all good outlaws.

Huck started a fire against the trunk of a fallen tree and fried some bacon for their supper. Feasting in the forest, the three pirates said they would never return to civilization. When they had devoured the last, crisp slices of bacon, they stretched out on the grass around the campfire.

"This is the life," laughed Tom. "Fresh air, good food, and no need to worry about washing or going to school."

"Paradise," agreed Joe.

"So, what do pirates do?" asked Huck, thoughtfully.

"It's plain sailing," Tom explained. "They steal ships and burn them, and bury the booty in desolate, ghostly spots, and make their prisoners walk the plank."

"Sounds like fun," sighed Huck. "But I reckon I'll get down to some snoozing, and you can tell me the rest in the morning."

The three pirates closed their eyes under the starry sky, and drifted off to sleep.

Tom woke at first light to the music of birdsong. He roused his friends and they went swimming in the warm shallows of the river. Their raft had vanished – carried off by a current or a swell in the river – but the loss of their ship didn't worry the pirates. Tom was thrilled that the last link to the civilized world had been torn away.

They returned to the camp refreshed and ravenous. While Huck got the fire going, the others dangled some lines in the water. To Tom's amazement, they had soon caught five, plump fish. Huck fried them for breakfast and Tom thought they were the most delicious fish he'd ever tasted.

After breakfast, they set out to explore the island. They went swimming every hour and it was noon before they got back to their camp. After a meal of cold ham, they chatted under the trees. But their conversation was interrupted by a booming sound that echoed from the other side of the island.

"What could it be?" cried Joe.

"It's not thunder," said Huck. "There's no sign of any storm."

"Let's take a look," suggested Tom.

They sprang up and ran across to some bushes overlooking the water. The town ferryboat was drifting downriver and its deck was crowded with people. At first, Tom and the boys couldn't guess what was happening, but suddenly, a jet of white smoke burst from the side of the ferryboat. The explosion of a cannon shot reached their island a few seconds later.

"Somebody's drowned," cried Tom. "They shoot a cannonball over the top of the water, and it brings the body floating up."

"I wish I was over there to see the cannon," said Joe.

"Me too," sighed Huck. "I'd like to know who it is they're looking for."

It was Tom who guessed the answer.

"Boys, I know who's drowned," he laughed. "We have."

In an instant, they were shouting and cheering with joy.

"We must be the talk of the town," yelled Tom.

The pirates strolled back to camp, chuckling and enjoying their fame. They caught more fish for their supper and then talked for hours, trying to guess what the townsfolk might be saying about them. But, when night shadows closed around the camp, the boys grew homesick and unhappy. Joe almost sniffled, and even Huck was quiet and moody.

When Huck and Joe dropped off to sleep, Tom lay watching them for them a long time in the firelight. At last, he got to his feet, silently, and hunted around for two pieces of white bark to write on. He scribbled a message across each piece, tucked one inside Joe's hat and the other into his jacket, and then tiptoed into the dark.

Five minutes later, Tom was swimming across the narrow channel of water that ran between the island and the riverbank. He waded ashore and started picking his way through the woods, making for the ferry landing opposite the town. It was coming up to ten o'clock when he reached the landing. Everything was quiet under the stars as Tom swam out to a little boat, or skiff, that was tied to the stern of the ferry. He grabbed the oarlocks and pulled himself over the side.

A bell rang and Tom heard the shout he'd been waiting for: "It's ten, cast off." Moments later, the skiff lurched and its prow lifted up, riding on the ferry's wake. After a voyage lasting fifteen minutes, the ferry stopped and Tom darted into the water. He scrambled ashore downstream from the landing, avoiding any strolling passengers.

Speeding through the alleyways, Tom quickly arrived at his aunt's back fence and peered in through the rear window. Aunt Polly, Sid, Mary and Joe Harper's mother were sitting in a group, talking. They were on the far side of the bed that stood next to the back door. Tom crept to the door and lifted the latch slowly and softly until the door swung open a crack.

"Why's the candle spluttering?" said Aunt Polly. "Make sure the door's closed will you, Sid?"

Tom heard his aunt's words and crawled through the open door and under the bed before Sid could spot him.

"As I was saying," Aunt Polly sighed, when Sid had returned to his place, "he wasn't a *bad* boy, exactly, just mischievous. He had a good heart."

"It was the same with my Joe," sobbed the other woman. "He was a kind boy, on the whole. To think that I whipped him for taking that cream, forgetting that I'd thrown it out the night before, because it tasted sour." And she burst into tears.

"I hope he's gone to *the good place*," said Sid. "But he always had the devil in him."

"That's enough," cried Aunt Polly, fiercely. "Don't say another word against your brother. The Good Lord is looking after him now."

Everyone in the room was snuffling and sad, and even Tom was beginning to feel a bit weepy, but he went on listening. He soon learned that the people in the town thought the boys must have gone swimming and drowned. When the Sheriff found the raft, washed up on the far shore, he guessed that the boys had tumbled into the water as they attempted a crossing. The middle of the river was deep and fast flowing, and most people thought the bodies were lost forever. It was Wednesday evening. If the boys were still missing on Sunday morning, the townsfolk would give up any hope that they might be alive and hold a funeral service.

Mrs. Harper dried her tears and said goodnight to Tom's family. Sid and Mary kissed Aunt Polly and climbed the stairs to their rooms, crying with all their hearts.

When she was alone, Tom's aunt got down on her knees and prayed for her missing boy. She spoke with such a feeling of love in her old, trembling voice that Tom's cheeks were wet with tears before she had finished.

He waited a long time for her to lie down and stop moaning. When he was sure she had fallen asleep, Tom got up from the floor and stood by the candle watching her. He took out his bark parchment and placed it by her pillow. But, as he turned to leave, he smiled at a sudden thought and put the bark message back into his pocket. Before leaving the room, he bent over and kissed his aunt gently on the lips.

Tom knew that the ferry had shut for the night, but he helped himself to the skiff and rowed a mile across the river. It was hard work at the oars, but Tom arrived safely at the landing an hour before dawn.

He tied up the skiff and rested in the grass. The sun was up by the time he was opposite the island, and he rested again before swimming across to the camp. Dripping and exhausted, he stepped between the trees, stopping and hiding when he heard the voices of his friends.

"Tom won't abandon us, don't you worry," said Joe. "He's a true pirate."

"I'm not worried," answered Huck. "The note says he'll be back for breakfast."

"Which he is," shouted Tom, charging into the camp. "And I've got plenty to tell you."

In the afternoon they hunted for turtle eggs along the shore of their island. Tom took fifty eggs out of one hole in the sand. The boys stuffed themselves with scrambled eggs for their dinner, and had dozens left over for breakfast on Friday. Then they swam and warmed themselves in the sun.

But as twilight settled over their island, all three pirates started thinking of home. Joe and Huck went off to stare across the water towards the lights of St. Petersburg. When they returned, Tom sensed there was mutiny in the air.

"I want to go back," Joe declared. "I'm getting lonely."

Tom was feeling homesick too, but he wanted the pirate gang to stay on the island for another day or two. He had only revealed part of his adventure in the town, and had been working on a dazzling plan.

"What about the fishing and the swimming?" he asked, trying to rally his troops. "It's the best we've ever had."

"Swimming's more fun when there's someone telling you not to do it," snapped Joe.

"What kind of pirate are you?" replied Tom. "I bet you miss your mother, you big baby."

"Yes, I do miss her," sobbed Joe. "And you'd miss your mother too, if you had one. I'm going back."

Joe picked up his clothes and began to dress. Tom stared across at Huck and asked: "How about you, old friend?"

"It *is* lonely out here," whispered Huck. "I reckon I'll be going back too."

Tom watched as Huck stood up and collected his things. The two deserters pleaded with Tom to join them. But when he flatly refused, they said their goodbyes and turned to go.

"Wait a minute, boys," Tom shouted, at the last moment. "I've been working on a scheme I think you'll like. Stay a while, and hear me out."

When Huck and Joe heard Tom's plan, they whooped and punched the air.

"You're a genius, Black Tom," cried Joe. "But why didn't you say something to us about it before?"

"I was still working on the details," said Tom,

modestly. "But I couldn't let you leave now, when we're so close to glory."

"We're staying," laughed Huck. "And I think we should smoke on it. I've got some pipes and tobacco in my sack."

Huck was an experienced smoker, unlike Tom and Joe who had never tasted tobacco. But the two novices sucked hard on the pipes he passed them, grinning with excitement.

"It's so easy," said Tom, trying not to gag on the smoke. "I reckon I'll light a pipe every day from now on."

"Me too," coughed Joe. "I've never felt better."

Huck took off his hat, dropping it on Tom's head, and stretched himself out, leaning against a tree while he puffed gently on his pipe. Black Tom gulped and fell silent. His stomach churned and his mouth watered. After a few minutes, the Terror of the Seas staggered to his feet.

"Boys," he muttered, feebly. "I think I've lost my knife, over in those bushes. I'd better go and look for it."

"I'll help you," cried Tom, standing and swaying. "I'll search on the other side of the camp."

Huck jumped up and offered to help.

"That's all right, Huck," Tom replied. "You stay here and take it easy. The two of us will find it."

So Huck sat down, and waited an hour. At last, he started feeling lonely and went searching for his comrades. They were lying in the woods, both pale and fast asleep. Huck chuckled, and left them in peace.

After midnight, Joe woke up and sniffed the air. He quickly roused the others.

"There's a storm coming," he warned. "The air's all wet and hot."

The three pirates huddled together by the fire, listening to the first, distant thunder roll of the approaching storm. They stared at the swaying branches of the trees as the wind picked up. When the first, white flash of lightning crackled around their island, it lit up three terrified faces. The next lightning burst seemed to explode directly over their heads, and a heavy rain began to fall.

"Run for the tent," Tom shouted.

They stumbled through a curtain of rain to the supply tent, as the tempest roared around them. But, a few seconds later, the wind ripped the old sail from its fastenings and snatched it away. Holding hands and soaked to the skin, the boys made a dash for the shelter of an old oak tree on the riverbank. The lightning flamed in the sky, and the pirates watched in horror as giant trees came crashing to the ground. But their chosen oak tree was sturdy, and it stood firm against the storm.

When the wind and the rain had finally died down, they hurried back to their camp to survey the damage.

The campfire, their supplies and beds were all sodden and strewn with broken branches. But Huck found a spark of fire still burning under the trunk of a toppled tree. He coaxed it back to life and the pirates built a great bonfire. They feasted on the remains of the ham and told each other yarns until dawn arrived – storm survivors retelling their adventures. When the warming sun slanted over the island, they wandered down to the shore and curled up to sleep in the sand.

On Sunday morning, the church bell in St. Petersburg tolled for the town's lost boys. The townsfolk gathered, and nobody could remember when the church had been so full. There was silence as Aunt Polly entered the hall, followed by Sid and Mary. The Harper family came in behind them, all dressed in black.

The grieving families walked slowly to the pews at the front of the church. To the sound of muffled sobs, the preacher began his sermon. He reminded the congregation of the boys' sweet and generous natures, and then described some of their escapades. There wasn't a dry eye in the room as the preacher ended his sermon, and even he was crying in the pulpit.

A sudden creak from the church door startled him. He looked up and let out a gasp. The whole congregation followed the preacher's gaze to the rear of the church – and saw the three pirates marching down the aisle. Tom was in the lead, striding along with his chest stuck out and his chin lifted high. Joe came next, beaming with joy, and Huck followed after him, looking rather sheepish. The boys had spent the night hiding in the church gallery, and woke to listen to their own funeral sermon.

The mourning families threw themselves on Tom and Joe and smothered them with kisses. Huck stood awkwardly at the edge of the group, and was about to slip away when Tom caught him by the hand.

"Aunt Polly, it's not fair," Tom shouted. "Somebody has to be glad to see Huck. He's back from the dead."

"So they do," she cried, and she hugged and kissed poor Huck until he was choking for air.

Suddenly the preacher shouted at the top of his voice: "Praise the Lord for returning our boys. Let's SING."

They sang until they shook the rafters.

Taking the Punishment

Tom Sawyer and his fellow pirates were the talk of the town after their return from the wilderness. Aunt Polly was so overcome with joy and relief to have Tom back, she barely scolded him for running away.

"You're home, and that's all that matters," she told him over breakfast the following morning. "But don't ever let me think you're dead and gone again. That was the worst part of it, worrying you were drowned. Why didn't you send me a message, to say that you were safe?"

"I tried," Tom replied. "I came over one night to leave you a note I'd written on a piece of bark. It said we were playing pirates and we'd be home soon. But when I heard about the funeral, I decided to wait and make a grand entrance. I'm sorry if I hurt you, Aunt Polly, I really am."

"Well, at least you thought of me," Aunt Polly chuckled, "before you started cooking up one of your schemes. You test me to my limits, Tom Sawyer, but I thank the good Lord that you're home. Now, take yourself off to school, before I get all weepy again."

Tom strolled towards school, basking in his notoriety as the daredevil leader of the runaways.

There wasn't a boy in the town that didn't envy him his pirate adventure. At the school playground a group of younger students flocked around him, proud to be seen standing next to Black Tom. When Becky Thatcher arrived, and smiled in his direction, Tom saw his chance for revenge. He pretended not to notice her friendly glances, and moved away to talk with another group of boys and girls.

"Tell me about the storm on your island," cried a girl called Amy, grabbing hold of Tom's hand. "Joe said it sounded like the end of the world was coming."

"It was a lot worse than that," boasted Tom. "If I hadn't locked my arms around that oak tree, we'd have been blown all the way to China."

While Tom bragged about saving Huck and Joe, Becky stepped over to the group. She laughed, nervously, and tried to start a conversation with one of the girls.

"Oh hello, Mary," she giggled. "I've got some news for everybody."

Tom didn't turn or even glance over his shoulder. Instead, he started telling Amy about his adventures with the ferryboat. But an excited crowd was growing around Becky.

"I'm having a picnic, when school closes for the summer," she announced. "My mother says I can invite all my friends, and anyone who *wants* to be my friend."

The message was clear, but Tom ignored Becky's offer and walked coolly away, leading Amy by the hand. Becky's lips trembled. She wanted to cry, but she forced herself to keep smiling in front of the other students. When the group drifted apart, she ran and hid behind some trees to sob for her lost Romeo. The tears burned her cheeks, until her sadness turned to rage and she began plotting a revenge of her own.

At the lunch break, Tom hurried over to Amy and asked if he could hold her hand. Poor Amy swooned and accepted. She never guessed Tom's cruel plan to make Becky jealous, as they circled the playground like sweethearts. But Tom's scheme backfired when he spotted his angel sitting on a bench and staring at a picture book with a rival. It was Alfred, the new boy in fancy clothes that Tom had thrashed at the start of the summer.

Tom's blood ran hot with jealousy as he stared at the two lovebirds. Becky didn't look up from the book, but she moved a little closer to her new admirer. She knew full well that Tom was watching, and was enjoying every second of his agony.

"If only it was another boy," Tom hissed under his breath. "I can't bear to see her sitting with that dandy."

"What's that, Tom?" chirped Amy, holding his fingers tighter.

But Tom only shook his head and yanked his hand away. "I've got to get home for lunch," he mumbled, and stormed off towards the gate.

Becky's fascination with Alfred's picture book quickly faded after Tom left the scene. She started to worry that she had gone too far, and that Tom would never forgive her for sitting with another boy. Alfred tried to interest her in a new chapter, but she only snapped at him: "Oh, don't bother me with any more silly drawings. Can't you see I'm upset?"

"But it was you who asked to see my book," he whimpered.

"Leave me alone," said Becky coldly, and burst into tears before running away.

Alfred stopped in his tracks, wondering what he had done to offend the girl. It didn't take long for him to guess the truth. Feeling humiliated and angry that Becky had duped him, he went back to the empty classroom to return his book. Tom's spelling book lay open on one of the other desks. Alfred snatched it up and poured ink across the pages.

"That should earn you a caning," he chuckled, as he closed the book and placed it back on the desk.

Becky had been passing at the window, and she witnessed Alfred's act of sabotage. She tiptoed away, thinking she could catch up with Tom and tell him everything. But, she quickly changed her mind. The sudden memory of Tom snubbing her in the playground made her furious, and she decided to keep silent and let him suffer.

Tom bounded into the schoolyard after lunch, feeling refreshed and cheerful. He ran straight up to Becky. "I was mean today," he told her, "and I want to say sorry. I played a sneaky trick on you and I'll never do it again, as long as I live. Can we be friends?"

Becky was taken aback by his gentle words, but she was still too angry to forgive him.

"Keep away from me, Tom Sawyer," she snapped spitefully. "I never want to speak to you again." She tossed her head and walked away, leaving Tom too stunned to reply.

When he'd recovered his wits he flew into a rage and chased after her.

"You're a merciless old witch, Becky Thatcher," he declared. "And you don't deserve my friendship."

Becky threw back an insult and charged off. She couldn't wait to hear the peel of the bell, and to see Tom flogged for the ruined spelling book.

As soon as the schoolmaster came out into the yard with his bell, Becky darted into the classroom. She wanted a *ringside* seat for Tom's caning. But, when she stepped past the master's desk, Becky noticed something that made her gasp. The master had left his desk drawer open, and Becky could just see the edge of the mysterious book he kept locked away there. When the class was busy with a test or written work, he sometimes retrieved this book and flicked through its pages. Some of the students whispered that it contained scandalous pictures. Everyone at the school was desperate to discover what the master was reading, but the book was always locked away in the desk at the end of class.

With a quick glance over her shoulder to check that she was alone, Becky reached down, seized the book and began flicking through its pages. She was disappointed to discover that it was nothing but an expensive, medical textbook and that most of its pictures were of skeletons.

A shadow fell across the page and Becky whirled around. Tom Sawyer stood in the doorway, staring at her in astonishment. Becky snatched at the book to close it, and in her hurry she ripped one of the pages.

"Look what you made me do, Tom," she cried, dropping the book into the drawer and slamming it shut. "What are you doing, sneaking up on me?"

"I didn't even know you were in here," Tom replied.

"I bet you'll tell on me," she shouted. "And I'll be whipped. But I know something awful that's going to happen to you. You wait and see."

Tom scratched his chin and tried to make sense of what she had said. He had no intention of telling the master anything, and he didn't want to see her punished. But he knew what the master's tactic would be when nobody confessed to the crime. He would ask each child in turn if they were the guilty party. Unlike Tom, Becky had no natural talent for deception. When the master posed his question, she would burst into tears and confess everything.

"She's in a tight spot, all right," Tom whispered to himself. "But I wonder if she'd help me out, if the situation was reversed?"

Tom couldn't concentrate on his studies that afternoon. He kept glancing over towards Becky's side of the room, trying to think up some scheme that might save her. His attentions were diverted when the master collected their books and discovered the ink on Tom's spelling test. Tom's denials and protests were vigorous, but useless. He swore that he was innocent, although in truth, Tom thought it was quite possible he had spilled the ink weeks ago and forgotten all about it. Becky waited for the inevitable beating, wondering if she should save him by telling on Alfred. But she kept quiet. "Why should I help him," she thought to herself, "when he's bound to tell on me?"

Tom took his whipping bravely and returned to his seat.

An hour drifted by, and then the master gave the class a test and reached into his desk for his book. Tom glanced over at Becky's ashen face. All thoughts of their earlier quarrels vanished and he felt a sudden, and unexpected urge to help her.

"Class!" growled the master, rising from his seat. "Who tore this book?"

Nobody made a sound. In the silence, the master scanned the room, searching for a blush or a blinking eye.

"Was it you, Benjamin Rogers?" he roared.

"No, sir."

"Or you, Joseph Harper?"

Joe shook his head. The master turned his probing stare towards the girls.

"Amy Lawrence, do you have anything to say?

"Nothing, sir," whispered Amy.

The girl behind Amy was Becky. Tom saw her trembling in terror.

"Rebecca Thatcher," boomed the master. "Look me in the eyes, girl. Did you tear this book?"

Tom jumped to his feet and shouted: "It was me."

He stepped forward to take the punishment, relishing the look of gratitude and adoration in Becky's eyes. "Seeing that is worth a hundred floggings," he told himself, as the master fetched the cane.

She waited after school for him, and whispered in his ear: "Tom, how *could* you be so noble?"

THE TRIAL

In July the school closed for the summer vacation and Tom was a free man. For two weeks he happily fished, played and swam, and then a terrible gloom swept over him. Becky Thatcher had to leave town on a visit to her relatives in the country. She would not return until the end of the summer, to host the picnic for her classmates.

Tom mooched along the riverbank and wandered alone through the woods. His daytime miseries soon spilled into his nights, and the dreadful secret of the murder haunted his dreams. With his body weakened by heartache and lack of sleep, Tom grew sick. Aunt Polly almost fainted when the doctor gave her the bad news. Tom had measles.

For five long weeks, he was feverish and confined to bed, like a prisoner locked away from the world. He was so ill, he lost all track of time and events. When he was finally well enough to stand, Tom staggered out into the blazing sun and went looking for his friend, Huck Finn. Tom had heard alarming whispers from Sid and Mary; the murder trial was coming to court.

Tom led Huck deep into the woods, to find a lonely spot where they would not be overheard.

"Well, have you told anyone?" Tom whispered.

"Told what?" replied Huck.

"Our secret."

"Of course not," cried Huck. "I signed the blood oath, didn't I?"

"Not one word, to anybody?" asked Tom.

"Listen to me, Tom Sawyer," said Huck, firmly. "I'm not a fool. If our secret got out, we'd be dead before nightfall. You know that, don't you?"

"I do," sighed Tom. "But I reckon we're safe, as long as we keep *mum*. But let's swear again, to make sure of it."

"Agreed," said Huck, and he joined Tom in repeating their oath.

"So, what's the talk going around?" Tom asked. "I've been down with the measles for over a month. Have I missed anything?"

"The talk is all about Muff Potter being the killer," Huck replied. "And it gives me the jitters every time I think about it."

"Me too," Tom declared. "I reckon Potter's a goner," he added, sadly. "Don't you feel sorry for him, sometimes?"

"All the time," answered Huck. "He's a drunk, but he's never hurt anybody that I know about. All he did was go fishing and sell his catch for whiskey. And he loafed around a lot, but who doesn't? I reckon he's a good man, at heart. He gave me half a fish once, when I was starving hungry."

"He mended my kite for me a few times," said Tom, guiltily. "I wish we could get him out of that brick prison."

"But we can't," replied Huck, sharply. "And they'd only catch him again if we did."

"I know," said Tom. "But I hate to hear people call him a bloodthirsty killer, when we know it's a lie."

The boys talked long into the afternoon, but it brought them no comfort. They were trapped with their secret, too scared of Injun Joe to reveal the truth and save Potter. As twilight settled over the woods, they strolled towards home, passing close to the prison.

"Let's give him some tobacco," Huck suggested.

They hurried over to the hut and Tom called out: "Anybody home?"

"Hey there," Potter answered. "I'm still here. Is Huck with you?"

"He is," replied Huck.

"So, what have you brought me today?" Potter chuckled, pushing his fingers between the bars. The boys often visited the prisoner, and always took him a gift. Huck passed him the tobacco and matches and they heard Potter sigh: "Boys, you're my only friends in the world. I thank you."

The man's heartfelt gratitude made Tom and Huck feel treacherous and cowardly.

"All the other boys have forgotten about me," said Potter. "But not you two. And that's how you know who your true friends are, boys. True friends stand by you when you get into trouble. I did a bad thing, a terrible thing, but you've stood by me. I must have been drunk and crazy when I did it. And now, I have to swing from a rope. Stay away from the whiskey, boys, and you won't end up in this hole, like me. Now Tom, climb up on Huck's back. I want to shake your hand."

Tom clambered up and stretched his arm into the darkness of the cell. Potter shook his hand, gently.

"Helping hands," Potter sighed. "I thank you boys."

Tom went home in a black mood, and his dreams that night were full of horrors. On the following day, he found himself drawn towards the courtroom building, where the trial had already started. He waited on the steps, fighting an impulse to rush inside and tell everything he knew. When anyone left the building, Tom shadowed them, listening for scraps of gossip. The things he heard were not encouraging. Injun Joe had repeated his story on the witness stand and it seemed certain that the jury would find Potter guilty. The trial was moving ahead so quickly, their verdict was expected in the morning.

Tom stayed out late that night and it was past midnight when he hoisted himself through the window of his room. His mind was buzzing with excitement and he was restless and twitching for hours, before he finally managed to sleep.

All the people of the town flocked to the courthouse that morning, anxious to see the murderer condemned. After a long wait the jury shuffled in and took their places. Potter arrived next, chained and cuffed, pale and hopeless. He stared down at the floor, trying to hide from the curious eyes of the townsfolk.

Injun Joe watched his wretched friend impassively, from his seat at the front of the court.

There was another pause until the judge arrived.

"Court is open," announced the Sheriff. "Counsel for the prosecution, call your first witness."

A man stepped forward and took the oath of honesty, with his palm resting across the court Bible. He testified that he had seen Muff Potter washing in a stream just before dawn.

"That's good enough for me," declared the lawyer. "Your witness."

"No questions," snapped Potter's lawyer.

The next witness had discovered the knife lying beside the doctor's corpse.

"Your witness," barked the prosecuting lawyer.

"Again, no questions," came the reply.

A third witness swore that he had seen Potter with the same knife. Everyone in the court could see that the prosecuting lawyer was trying to establish a solid link between the murder weapon and the murderer.

"No questions," said Potter's lawyer.

There was a murmur from the crowd and even the judge raised an eyebrow. Potter's lawyer seemed to be making no effort to save his client from the hangman's noose. The pattern was repeated as several witnesses took the stand to testify about Potter's guilty confession at the graveyard. Potter's lawyer refused to question any of them.

"There is no possibility of doubt in this trial," declared the prosecuting lawyer, and he pointed towards Potter. "This man is the murderer. We rest our case."

Potter groaned and pressed his face into his shackled hands. Slowly, his lawyer stepped into the middle of the courtroom.

"Judge, and jury," he began. "At the start of this trial, I told you that my purpose was to ask you to show mercy to my client. I hoped to prove that Muff Potter was drunk and not in his right mind when he fought with the unfortunate doctor. But new evidence has come to light, and I wish to change that plea. Muff Potter is innocent. I call Tom Sawyer."

Every eye in the room turned on Tom as he took his place on the stand. His fingers trembled as he placed them on the Bible for the oath.

"Thomas Sawyer," asked the lawyer. "Were you in the graveyard, on the night of the doctor's murder?"

Tom glanced towards Injun Joe's iron face and his tongue failed him. The audience listened in a breathless hush, until Tom summoned the courage to whisper: "I was."

"A bit louder, please," instructed the lawyer. "Don't be afraid."

"I was there," said Tom, boldly.

A horrible smile flashed across Injun Joe's lips.

"Were you near Hoss Williams' grave?"

"Yes, I was."

"Tell me, exactly, where were you?"

"I was hiding behind the elm trees, at the edge of the grave."

Injun Joe leaned forward in his chair. His massive fists were clenched tight.

"Tell me what happened," said the lawyer.

"I saw it all," replied Tom.

There was a gasp from the back of the courtroom and the judge called for quiet.

"Muff Potter and the doctor started fighting," Tom continued. "As the doctor hit Potter, Injun Joe jumped in with the knife…"

There was a crash as Injun Joe exploded out of his chair. He brushed aside the Sheriff and his deputy and hurled himself through a window. The killer was gone.

A Treasure Chest

Tom was a hero once again after saving Potter. He was the darling of the old and the envy of the young. The town newspaper even published a story describing his bravery on the witness stand, and some of the younger boys said he'd make a fine President – if he decided not to run off and be a pirate again.

The world is a fickle place, as Potter quickly discovered. Men and women from the town hugged and praised him just as violently as they had abused him in the past. But that sort of conduct is what makes the world a good place to live in, and there were no complaints from Potter.

Tom's days passed in a blur of handshakes, smiles and warm congratulations, but in the nights he was alone with his dreams. Injun Joe stalked him in his nightmares, until Tom tore at the sheets and screamed for help.

Nothing could persuade him to leave the safety of the house after dark. Huck was in the same state of terror, although his name had not been mentioned in court. Tom had confessed everything to Potter's lawyer the night before the trial, and asked him to keep Huck's part in the story a secret. But Huck had little faith in the promise of a stranger, when his best friend had broken a solemn oath of silence.

Huck fretted that Injun Joe would guess that Tom had not been alone in the graveyard, and expected to feel the killer's steely fingers closing around his neck at any second.

"We won't be safe until he's dead," Tom said to Huck one day. "And I'll want to see his corpse before I believe it."

The Sheriff posted a reward and searched the countryside, but there was no trace of the murderer. Injun Joe had gone to ground.

Despite his bad dreams and fears, Tom was soon seized by a raging passion that filled him with new energy: treasure-hunting. He dashed around town, trying to find partners who could help with the digging. Only Huck Finn was ready and willing to wield a shovel. Huck was always hungry for a new adventure.

"Where do we dig for this treasure?" he asked, impatiently.

"Just about anywhere you like," Tom replied.

"Do you mean it's buried all around us?" cried Huck.

"Oh no," said Tom, seriously. "It's hidden in all the strangest places. Pirates bury it on islands, in rotten chests that fall apart when you try to lift them. Outlaws prefer haunted houses. They put their gold in the garden or under the floorboards, and say a curse over it before they ride off into the night."

"But why do they hide it?" asked Huck. "If I had any money I'd spend it and have a good time."

"So would I," laughed Tom. "But robbers don't think like us. They always stash their money and leave it alone for years."

"So, when do they come back for it?" asked Huck.

"Most times they forget where it is," Tom explained. "Or they die before they can remember. And the gold gets rusty and dusty, until somebody finds an old map that says where it is, written on a yellow piece of paper."

"Is it always yellow?"

"Always," Tom declared. "And it's covered in secret marks and codes that the treasure hunter has to decipher before it leads him to the booty."

"Do you have a piece of yellow paper?" asked Huck.
"No."

"Well, how do we find the booty?" Huck protested.

"I've been through that already," replied Tom, a bit sharply. "People with treasure to hide always pick islands or haunted houses. Well, we've tried Jackson's Island and we didn't see anything buried there, so I thought we could try digging around some haunted houses."

"I can only think of one," said Huck. "It's that tumbledown cabin up near Cardiff Hill."

"That's the same one I was thinking of," Tom answered. "And I know where we can find a pick and a shovel. Let's get going."

It took the treasure hunters more than an hour to climb through the thick woods of Cardiff Hill and they were panting and hot before they reached the top. Tom glimpsed the house first, standing alone in a dark tangle of bushes and small fruit trees. It was a sorry sight, with a crumbling chimney and one corner of its roof caved in. Weeds sprouted in its open doorway and the window shutters were splintered and hanging loose.

"I don't like haunted houses," whispered Huck, flopping into the grass. "And I never wanted any dealings with ghosts and goblins. Perhaps we should turn back?"

"They won't mind us digging around the garden in the daytime," replied Tom, shakily.

"I suppose not," sighed Huck. "But I've heard

stories about blue lights flashing past those windows when it gets dark. We'll have to leave at twilight."

"Agreed," said Tom, and he lay down against a tree to catch his breath.

"Hey, Huck," asked Tom, as they stumbled through the bushes towards the house. "What do you plan to do with your share of the treasure?"

"I'll have a big steak and a glass of soda every day," laughed Huck. "And I'll buy a ticket to get into the circus, instead of slipping under the canvas."

"Won't you save any of it?"

"What for?" cried Huck.

"For a rainy day," replied Tom. "And to have something to live on when you get old."

"That wouldn't work," sighed Huck. "Pap would come back to town and get his claws into it, if I didn't spend it in a hurry. What are you going to do when you're rich?"

"I'll buy myself a new drum, and a bulldog and a red neck-tie. I might even get married."

"Married?" coughed Huck. "Are you out of your right mind?"

"What's wrong with getting married?"

"Just about everything's wrong with it," explained Huck. "Look at Pap and my mother. They used to fight like wild cats, day and night."

"The girl I'm going to marry won't fight," Tom replied, proudly.

"Women are all born fighters," answered Huck. "And I'll bet she's no different. What's her name?"

"Well, I don't want you making fun of her," replied Tom, a little hurt. "I'll tell you another time."

"Don't do it, Tom," Huck pleaded. "I'll be the loneliest boy in the country if you run off and get married."

"Oh, you don't have to worry about that," answered Tom, soothingly. "I'll build a big house with all my gold and you can come and live with us."

"That's a fine idea," replied Huck. "I knew you wouldn't forget about me."

"Of course I won't," said Tom. "Now let's get digging. We've got to find the treasure before we can spend it."

There was a plot of broken earth to the front of the house – an old garden now covered in weeds and brambles. Tom looked up at the branches of an overhanging tree, selected a likely spot and the boys started hacking at the ground.

"Do they always bury it this far down?" asked Huck, when the hole was so deep it came up to his waist.

"No," answered Tom. "I reckon we should try in another place."

They moved off to the right and, once again, Tom checked the tree and told Huck where to dig.

"What are you studying that tree for?" Huck asked, mystified.

"Some pirates bury their gold under the shadow of a branch, as a marker," replied Tom. "But they use a moonlight shadow, of course, when the ghosts and demons are out."

"But moonlight shadows are different from daytime shadows," snapped Huck. "They change shape with every passing hour. Do you mean to say we've been following the wrong shadows?"

"I guess that's why we haven't found the treasure," sighed Tom.

Huck dropped his shovel in the dirt.

"We don't have the yellow paper, and we don't have the right shadows," he said, in disgust. "So, how are we going to get rich?"

"We could look in the house," whispered Tom.

The boys glanced over at the black doorway of the cabin.

"It's still daylight," said Tom.

"I know, but twilight isn't far off," complained Huck.

"Let's just take a look. We don't have to go in."

They stepped over to the twisted boards around the porch of the house. Peering through the doorway, they could see a weed-choked, filthy room, an ancient fireplace and a leaning staircase. The walls were covered in cobwebs and sinister stains.

"Come on," whispered Tom, creeping into the gloom.

"You said we were just looking," hissed Huck.

"That's all we're doing," answered Tom.

"But there's nothing here," said Huck, following gingerly after his friend.

"Let's take a look upstairs," suggested Tom.

"What for?" hissed Huck.

"We won't know what's there if we don't look."

"You can go alone."

"Are you chicken?" asked Tom, with a chuckle.

Huck dropped their tools in a corner of the room and they started up the stairs. They came out into an empty space, with a tall closet standing off to one side.

"Let's open it up," said Tom.

"There might be a ghost in there," whispered Huck. "It's almost twilight outside and twice as dark in here."

Tom ignored his friend's warning and tugged at the closet door. There was nothing inside.

"Now we can get out of here," said Huck. "I've proved I'm not chicken."

"Quiet!" snapped Tom, and his face turned white as salt. "I heard something. Keep still, Huck. I think there's someone at the door."

The boys dropped to their knees and lay down on the dusty planks of the floor.

"They've stopped," whispered Tom, trying to peer through a knothole in one of the boards. "No, wait, I can hear footsteps. Don't make a sound, Huck. Don't even breathe."

Two men entered. The boys immediately recognized one of them as the old deaf and dumb Spaniard who had been hanging around town for a week or two. He wore a ragged poncho and a crumpled sombrero, and always protected his eyes with a pair of dark glasses. The other man was scruffy and rough-faced. He crossed the room and sat down on the dirt floor, facing the doorway.

"I don't like it," he grumbled. "I've thought it over and it's too dangerous."

"Are you a coward?" thundered the Spaniard, to the boys' amazement. They had never heard the man speak, but they recognized the voice in a flash. It was Injun Joe's. Tom had to bite hard on his lip to stop his teeth chattering with fear.

"The last job we did was just as dangerous," snapped Injun Joe. "And we got away with it. Look at the risks we're taking now, coming here in the daytime."

"I know that," replied the man. "But we had to talk, and I reckon the people in the town are too scared of this place to come snooping around, even in daylight."

"I hope you're right," snarled Injun Joe. "Let's have a bite to eat."

The two men fumbled in a sack they had brought with them, and were soon munching on hunks of bread and some dried meat.

"You'd better hide at the camp upriver," said Injun Joe, when he'd finished snacking. "You can wait there until I send for you. I'll take a risk and go back into town, to look the job over one last time. After we've done it, we'll run for Texas, together."

"That suits me," replied the other man. "I've had enough of this shack."

Injun Joe yawned and stretched his arms. "That's settled then," he said. "I'm dead tired, so let's get some rest. It's your turn to take the first watch."

He curled down into the weeds and in less than a minute he was snoring. His partner stared out into the woods, yawning and scratching his head. It wasn't long before his eyes closed and his breathing changed. He slumped to one side and began to snore too.

"Now's our chance," whispered Tom. "Let's go."

But Huck was too paralyzed with fear to move.

"I can't do it," he groaned. "If they wake up, they'll skin us alive."

Tom begged him to join him in the escape attempt, but Huck refused. At last, Tom rose and tiptoed over towards the top of the stairs. But, as he shifted his weight onto the first step, the board let out a loud *creak* that turned Tom's blood to ice. He hurried back and lay down next to his friend.

"We'll have to wait," he hissed.

"I'm all for that," Huck replied. "It'll be dark soon. We might stand a better chance of getting away then."

Without making a sound, Injun Joe suddenly sat bolt upright. He turned a grim smile towards the guard and gave him a kick.

"Wake up!" he growled. "A fine watchman you are. But don't worry, nothing's happened."

"Was I asleep?" asked the man, rubbing his cheeks.

"No, you were just resting your eyes," answered Injun Joe, sourly. "But it's time to get moving. What do you want to do with the swag we've got left over?"

"Leave it here, I reckon," replied the man. "There's no point in carrying it around with us before we leave for the South. Six hundred dollars in silver is quite a weight."

"All right," said Injun Joe. "We can come back here one last time."

"It's better to come at night," suggested the other man. "I don't like moving around too much in the daylight."

"That suits me," answered Injun Joe. "But it might be a few days, or longer, before we get back here. Let's bury the loot in a safer place."

"Good idea," said the man.

He walked across the room and lifted one of the hearthstones around the fireplace. Tom and Huck heard the music of coins jingling and watched as the man pulled out a moneybag. He took out a handful of coins and passed another handful to Injun Joe.

"For accidentals," he chuckled.

"Pass me the bag," ordered Injun Joe, without any hint of a smile.

He took the bag, slid a long knife from under his poncho and began scratching at the dirt in the corner of the room. Tom and Huck forgot all their fears as they watched the treasure sack dangling from Injun Joe's fist. They couldn't believe their luck. As soon as the men left the cabin, the boys would be rich. Six hundred dollars was enough to keep Huck in steak and soda pop for the rest of his life, and there would be enough left over to pay for Tom's wedding. They nudged and winked at each other, celebrating their good fortune.

Injun Joe's knife struck something hard.

"What's this?" he cried. "It feels like rotten wood."

Tom's mouth fell open.

"No," said Injun Joe again, "it's a box. My knife's punched a hole in it. I'll see what's inside."

He lifted out a handful of gleaming coins.

"Gold," whispered the other man. "It's full of gold. Let's dig it out. There's an old pick and a shovel leaning in the corner here."

He passed Injun Joe the boys' pick and shovel. Joe turned the shovel over in his hand and stared at the blade for a moment before starting to dig.

"I've got it free," he cried. "Help me drag it out."

The men pulled an old, wooden strongbox into the middle of the room. They smashed the lid open with the pick and sat contemplating their treasure in blissful silence. Ten feet above them, Huck and Tom feasted their eyes on the same sight.

"There must be thousands of dollars here," whispered Injun Joe.

"It could be the Murrel gang that left it here," gasped the other man. "I've heard stories about them hiding their swag in these parts."

"I've heard those stories too," said Injun Joe. "And I reckon we've found their lost gold."

"Well, now there's no need to risk our necks doing that job we were going to do," cried Joe's partner, clapping his hands.

But Joe frowned and slammed the lid.

"You don't know me very well," he hissed. "That job's more than a robbery to me. It's about revenge."

A wicked light flamed in his eyes. "We're not going to Texas until the job's done. Do you understand?"

"If that's what you want, I'll help you," replied the other man, timidly. "But what are we going to do with this treasure? Shall we bury it again?"

"Yes," answered Injun Joe.

The boys shook hands and Tom punched the air in delight.

"No!" Injun Joe suddenly roared and Tom's heart sank.

"There was something funny about that pick," he went on. "It had fresh earth on it."

The boys exchanged terrified glances.

"And what were those tools doing here, in the first place?" asked Injun Joe, slyly, rising to his feet. "Somebody must have carried them here, and they might come back. If they noticed that the ground had been disturbed, they'd find the treasure. No, we'll take it to my den."

"Which one?" asked the other man.

"Number two, under the cross."

"You're a smart one. It's already dark outside. Why don't we make a start?"

Injun Joe paced around the room, peering into every nook and cranny. "Who's been here?" he whispered to himself, lost in thought. Suddenly, he wheeled around to face his partner.

"Do you think they could be upstairs?"

Tom and Huck gulped together, and fought down the urge to scream. Tom tapped Huck on the shoulder and pointed towards the closet, but Huck was too scared to move a muscle. The boys listened in horror as Injun Joe walked towards the staircase.

"I'm going up there," he snarled, and they heard his boot scraping on the first step.

"Be careful, Joe," called the other man.

"I've got my knife," hissed Injun Joe, climbing higher.

Tom's heart was pounding so quickly he thought it would burst from his chest. He heard Injun Joe, almost at the top step, and then there was a *snap* and the rotten timbers supporting the staircase collapsed. Injun Joe landed in a heap of splinters, dust and broken boards. He jumped up, cursing.

"Nobody's been up there in a good few years," he declared. "Come on, we're wasting time."

Huck and Tom watched, with sadness and relief, as the two men lifted the box between them and hurried into the night.

ON THE HUNT

Tom woke late in the morning, still dreaming of ghosts, outlaws and treasure boxes brimming with gold.

"Silly dreams," he whispered, yanking the sheets over his head.

The next instant, he had torn the sheets away and was pulling on some clothes.

"Could it be true?" he mumbled, trying to clear his mind. Everything he remembered from the previous evening seemed so incredible, it had merged and melted into his dream fantasies. There was only one person he could think of who could set the matter straight. He gobbled his breakfast at breakneck speed and went in search of Huckleberry Finn.

Tom found his friend sitting on the wooden rail of a skiff, dangling his feet in the river and looking miserable. He decided to let Huck raise the subject of the treasure. If he said nothing about it, Tom would know it was only a fantasy adventure and he would be spared any embarrassment.

"Hello, Huck," called Tom.

"Hello, yourself," replied Huck.

There was silence for a full minute.

"Oh, Tom," said Huck, groaning, "why were we so stupid as to take those tools into the house? If Injun Joe hadn't spotted them, he would have left the treasure where he found it. It's just awful. I don't know if my heart can bear it."

"Then it's not a dream?" Tom cried with joy. "We did see that treasure?"

"Did you think it was a dream?" yelled Huck in disbelief. "If those stairs had been strong enough to carry the weight of a man, and not just a boy, you would have seen how much of a dream it was. While you've been dreaming, I've been having nightmares. And Injun Joe's in every one of them, coming after me with that big knife of his."

"We've got to find him," replied Tom, boldly. "He'll lead us to the gold."

"Are you crazy?" yelled Huck. "I'm staying away from that killer. The sooner he goes to Texas, the better."

"But he has to do that job first," gulped Tom. "He was talking about taking *revenge*. What do you think of that?"

"I think it's another man's problem," replied Huck, coldly.

"But what if he means *us*?" cried Tom.

"Don't say that," cried Huck, nearly fainting. "He must mean someone else."

"I hope so."

"And he doesn't know about me, does he?" whispered Huck. "You're the one he's after."

"That's right," replied Tom. "And I'll try not to mention your name when he puts the knife to my throat."

"Oh, I'm sorry," sighed Huck. "I'm so jumpy, I don't know what I'm saying. But what are we going to do?"

"Do you want a share in that treasure?"

"Of course I do," laughed Huck.

"Then we have to find the number two den," said Tom, calmly.

"It's a riddle to me. Where do *you* think it is?"

"It could be a house number," suggested Tom.

"That's a fine idea, but people don't use house numbers in St. Petersburg. Do you think the den's in another town?"

"No, it must be close to here," answered Tom. "It might be the number of a room."

"I think you've got it," shouted Huck, jumping up in his excitement. "They have room numbers in the two taverns."

"I know the boy that lives in one of them," cried Tom. "His father runs the place. You wait here while I find out who's staying in room number two. I'll be back inside an hour."

Tom raced into town and was soon questioning the puzzled son of the tavern keeper. The boy knew all the comings and goings around the two buildings. In the more expensive inn, a young lawyer had been renting room No.2 for several months. But the lodger in the other tavern was a mystery man who came and went in darkness.

"He leaves the rent out for us in the mornings," whispered the boy. "But nobody's ever set eyes on him.

I've seen strange lights flashing under the door, in the hours before dawn. It's almost as though that room's haunted by a ghost."

"It *must* be Injun Joe," cried Huck, when Tom had finished telling the story. "But now that we've found him, how do we go about stealing the treasure?"

"I've got a plan," said Tom, proudly. "My informer at the inn told me there's a back door to room No. 2. It opens onto an alleyway. We'll collect all the keys we can muster, and wait for a really dark night with no moonlight to betray us. Then we'll sneak down there and try to open the lock."

"But what about Injun Joe?"

"We'd better keep a lookout at the tavern for him," explained Tom. "Let's start tonight, taking watches in shifts. If you see him before I do, follow after him and he'll lead you straight to the treasure."

"Do I have to follow him all by myself?" gulped Huck.

"You'll be safe in the shadows," replied Tom. "And remember, he's got no reason to be suspicious of you."

"All right, Tom, I'll try to be brave."

"That's the talk," cried Tom. "Don't weaken, Huck, and we'll have our hands on that gold in no time at all."

The boys set out on their adventure that evening. They hung around the tavern until after nine, with Tom watching the entrance to the alleyway and Huck keeping an eye on the front of the building. There was no sign of the Spaniard, but because the night sky was clear and bright, Tom decided not to try the keys.

"I'm going home," Tom whispered to his friend. "If it gets dark soon, come and *meow* in the garden and I'll climb down to join you."

The sky remained clear. At midnight, Huck left his post and bedded down for the night in an empty sugar barrel.

For two more nights, the moon shone down on the alleyway and the boys had to delay the treasure hunt. On the fourth night, however, the sky was an inky black. Tom carried Aunt Polly's tin lantern, a ring of keys and a towel down to Huck's barrel. He lit the flame inside the lantern, and swaddled it with the towel. By moving the cloth to one side, Tom could shine a narrow beam of light, like a torch.

The boys stood watch for an hour, looking for any signs of life from room No. 2, but all was quiet. At midnight, Tom tiptoed into the gloom while Huck stood guard duty at the end of the alley.

Huck listened to his heart beating, staring into the dark for any glimmer from Tom's lantern. The night was eerily quiet, interrupted only by the occasional rumbling of distant thunder. Beads of ice-cold sweat dripped down Huck's back, and he had to clench his fists to stop his fingers from trembling. He took a step into the alleyway, wondering if Tom was hurt, or in trouble.

Suddenly, there was a flash of light and Tom came streaking out of the blackness.

"Run, Huck!" he cried. "Run for your life."

There was no need to repeat the warning. Huck was flying along like an express train before Tom could say another word. The boys didn't stop until they reached the shelter of the deserted tannery.

"It was awful," cried Tom, panting for air. "I tried two of the keys in the door, but they made a terrible scraping sound and wouldn't turn the lock. Then, I dropped the whole bunch of keys and had to lean forward on the door to reach down for them. But the door swung open and I stumbled inside. It wasn't even locked."

"So, what happened next?" gasped Huck.

"I almost stepped on Injun Joe's hand."

"He was there?" cried Huck.

"Stretched out and sound asleep, lying by the door. There was a whiskey bottle standing next to him so I reckon he'd been drinking until he'd passed out."

"And did you see the treasure box?"

"I didn't wait to look around, Huck," said Tom, crossly. "I had other things on my mind. Injun Joe could have sprung up at any second and slit my throat."

"But if he's drunk," pleaded Huck, "this might be the best time for you to search his room for the box."

"It's too risky," Tom replied, shaking his head. "I could knock something over and wake him. No, let's wait until we know he's left the room. We'll watch the tavern every night, and as soon as he steps out we'll snatch that box quicker than lightning."

"It's a good plan," Huck agreed. "There's no sense in taking risks. I'll do the watching, if you promise to do the other part of the job. You already know the lay of the land, so to speak."

"It's a deal," said Tom. "When you see him leave, run up to my house and *meow*. I'll slip out straight away. Will you watch for the rest of tonight?"

"Of course," Huck replied, bravely. "I'll be a watchman at night and sleep by day. I'll spy on that tavern for a year, if that's how long it takes for us to swipe the treasure."

"And where will I find you in the daytime?" asked Tom. "There's a storm coming tonight. You can't stay outside in that barrel. Is there anywhere else you can bed down?"

"Ben Rogers said I could use his hayloft," Huck answered. "It's dry and comfy there."

"I won't disturb you unless I have to," added Tom. "With any luck, the next time we'll meet is when I hear a cat singing at my window."

GOING UNDERGROUND

On Friday morning, Tom heard some news that made him forget all about Injun Joe and the missing treasure – Becky was back in town. He went looking for his sweetheart and spent the whole afternoon playing games with her and a crowd of their schoolmates. The day ended with more good news, when Becky persuaded her mother to let her host the long-promised picnic on the following morning. Tom helped Becky prepare the invitations and deliver them before sunset. At bedtime, most of the town children were too excited about the picnic to sleep, and Tom was no exception. He wrestled with the sheets, expecting to hear Huck's cat call from the garden at any second. Tom was longing to astonish Becky and the assembled picnickers with his treasure trove, but he was disappointed. No signal came that night.

Tom woke late and hurried to join a crowd of noisy, laughing children who had gathered outside Judge Thatcher's house. It was not the custom of the town to send parents along to spoil a party for the children. People thought the youngsters were safe enough with a small group of older brothers and sisters to act as escorts. At eleven o'clock, the young crowd tumbled along the main street, weighed down with baskets and rugs. They were making for the old ferryboat, which Mrs. Thatcher had charted to carry them a few miles downriver. There were only two familiar faces missing from the throng. Sid was sick with a fever and had to miss the fun, and Mary had volunteered to stay at home to keep him company.

Mrs. Thatcher had a last piece of advice for her daughter. "You'll be back home late, Becky. Perhaps you should spend the night with some of the girls that live by the ferry landing?"

"I will, Mamma," laughed Becky. "I can stay with Suzy Harper."

"Very well. And don't be any trouble to her parents."

Tom overheard this conversation, and he soon hit upon an idea to take advantage of Mrs. Thatcher's offer.

"We don't have to stay with the Harpers tonight," he whispered to Becky, as they rushed down the street. "Let's walk up the hill from the ferry. We can stop at Widow Douglas's place and eat some of her ice cream. She's always got ice cream, and she'd be glad to have some company."

"That sounds like fun," giggled Becky. "But what would Mamma say?"

"She'll never find out about it," replied Tom. "All she wants is for you to be safe for the night, and there's no safer place than the Widow's house. I reckon your mamma would say the same thing if she thought it over."

"You reckon?" Becky asked.

"I know she would. It's the most comfortable house in town, and it's full of ice cream."

"All right, Tom," said Becky, smiling. "But let's keep it a secret that we're planning to stay there. I don't want Mamma to hear anything."

Tom nodded and took Becky's hand. He was looking forward to tasting the Widow's ice cream, but a sudden thought made his heart sink. What would happen if Huck came with the alarm call that evening? For a moment, Tom considered going without the ice cream, but he quickly came to his senses.

"Huck didn't turn up last night," he muttered to himself. "So why should he come this evening?"

This logic was enough to satisfy Tom and he decided to put all thoughts of the treasure to the back of his mind. He had a picnic to enjoy.

After a short voyage, the ferryboat stopped and was tied up at the edge of some thick woods. A horde of children swarmed ashore and soon the forest was ringing with their shouts and laughter. They played among the trees and crags until they became ravenous and stormed back to the picnic camp. After a feast of sandwiches and lemonade, they lay in the wood's shade and chatted.

"Who's ready for McDougal's cave?" a boy suddenly shouted.

Every girl and boy jumped up, ready for a fresh adventure. Someone brought a box of candles from the ferryboat and the children scampered up a hill towards a break in the trees. The mouth of the cave was shaped like a letter *A*, carved into the hillside. A massive, oak door covered the entrance, but it had no lock and a group of the older boys heaved it open. Inside was a small chamber, as chilly as a winter morning. The walls were made of solid, glass-smooth limestone covered with a film of icy water.

It was a strange sensation to stand in the gloom and cold of the cave mouth, staring out at the green valley basking in the sun. But the children didn't linger over the view. They were too busy lighting candles, pushing, whistling and joking as they began their procession inside. The path they followed was only eight or ten feet wide, and new crevices and alleyways opened off it after every few steps. McDougal's Cave was a rock honeycomb, a vast labyrinth of crooked paths running into each other and leading nowhere.

Some of the old ferrymen said that a man could wander for days and never reach the end of it. The tunnels sloped down and down, leading the explorer through layer upon layer of endless labyrinths. No man claimed to know his way around the whole cave; everyone agreed this would be impossible. Most of the young men knew a portion of the rock maze, and they didn't wander out of it. Tom Sawyer knew as many of the cave's twists and turns as anyone.

The happy procession moved deeper into the cave and then small groups and couples began darting away into the shadows of the side tunnels. Children flew along the dismal, stone corridors, jumping out to surprise their friends where two alleyways joined. When they grew tired of this game, they formed teams and played hide-and-seek. Some teams hid themselves for up to thirty minutes in the vast network of tunnels, before they were discovered.

With the games over, groups of children began picking their way back to the mouth of the cave. They were smeared with clay and candle wax, panting and exhausted, but everyone was in good spirits. When they stepped out through the oak door, the children and were astonished to see that twilight had already settled over the woods. The ferryboat's signal bell had been clanging for half an hour, but the explorers had lost track of the time, deep in the bowels of the cave.

The children rushed through the trees and down to the riverbank, where the captain quickly helped them onboard. He was running late, and was so anxious to reach the town before nightfall he didn't bother to take a head count of his passengers. One of his crew pushed them away from the shore and a moment later the little boat was moving upstream.

HERO HUCK

Huckleberry Finn had already begun his watch over the tavern when the ferryboat chugged back into town. He saw the boat's lights, glinting on the water, but couldn't hear any sounds coming from the deck. The children were huddled together in silence, exhausted after their picnic adventure. Huck shook his head, puzzling over the boat's mystery cargo, and turned his attention back to the tavern.

The night turned cloudy and dark while Huck watched his town slowly going to sleep. By ten o'clock, the last wagon had creaked past, and bedroom lights in every house were winking out. There were no footsteps or whispers echoing along the streets. At eleven, the lights in the tavern went out and Huck was left alone with the quiet and the ghosts.

Huck waited an hour, but nothing happened. He began to yawn and rub his eyes, yearning for his soft mattress of straw in the barn, but as he was about to leave, a sudden noise turned his blood to ice. The door in the alleyway closed softly.

Huck pressed himself against the wall, hiding in the gloom. The next instant, two men brushed past him and Huck saw that one of them was clutching something heavy under his arm. Huck guessed it was the treasure box.

But if Injun Joe was moving the gold there was no time to run and warn Tom Sawyer. The bandits and their booty would be miles away before the boys got back to the tavern. Huck knew his only chance of capturing the gold was to follow the men to their new hideout. He hurried after them, keeping to the shadows and stepping as quietly as a cat.

The two figures quickly made their way to the outskirts of the town and took a path snaking towards Cardiff Hill. They passed the Welshman's house when they were halfway up the track.

"That's good," Huck whispered to himself. He was certain that Injun Joe would bury the treasure in the old quarry just below the summit of the hill. But Huck was mistaken. The men rushed by the entrance to the quarry, turned off the road and plunged into the thick woodland surrounding Widow Douglas' house.

Huck had to close his distance to stand any chance of keeping the men in sight. He trotted along a narrow path between the trees, stopping now and again to listen to the night sounds. After a few minutes, all he could hear was the beating of his own heart. There was no moonlight under the canopy of leaves and Huck could barely see his fingers in front of his face. An owl screeched and hooted over the hill, and he trembled as he listened to its lonely call.

A man cleared his throat next to him in the darkness and Huck's heart shot into his throat. Injun Joe was standing no more than an arm's length away, completely hidden in the dark.

"Curse her," said Injun Joe. "She must have company. I can see a light."

"I can't see any," said another voice in the blackness. It was the man from the haunted cabin.

Huck's skin tingled with fear as he guessed why Injun Joe was prowling through these woods. The killer had talked of staying in town and taking revenge on somebody, even after finding the gold. Widow Douglas must have been his target. Huck got ready to run, but before he could slip away he remembered how the Widow had always treated him kindly in the past. He wished there was some way that he could warn her, but he didn't dare sprint towards the house. Injun Joe would catch him before he was out of the wood, and skin him alive.

"Step towards me," growled Injun Joe and Huck heard the other man stumble around a bush.

"I see it now," said the man. "I reckon she does have company. We'd better forget about it."

"Forget it?" snapped Injun Joe. "But I'm leaving in the morning and never coming back. This is my last chance for revenge. I tell you again, you can have all the loot we find in the house. But I want her husband to get what's coming to him. When he was justice of the peace he *horsewhipped* me in front of the whole town. A man can't forgive something like that. He died before I could get my revenge, so instead, I'll take it out on *her*."

"I don't want anything to do with killing," cried the other man.

"Who said anything about killing?" laughed Injun Joe. "When you want revenge on a woman, you don't kill her. You take away her looks. When I finish with her, she'll be a monster. Her own child wouldn't recognize her."

"I want no part of it," squealed the other man.

"If you flinch, I'll kill you," hissed Injun Joe. "I'll shoot you down like a dog. I might need your help in the house."

The other man gulped. "If it has to be done," he

said weakly, "let's get on with it. I'm getting the shivers waiting out here in the woods."

"There's no hurry," replied Injun Joe, calmly. "We'll wait until the lights go out and then creep through an open window. The patient man gets the prize."

Huck sensed that the two men would be quiet now, and the thought of standing next to them in the deathly silence was too much for him to bear. He held his breath and took a step backwards, planting his foot firmly and carefully. On his fourth step, he heard a leaf crunch under his toes, but the noise didn't disturb the waiting killers. Huck turned his body, as slowly as a ship swinging around, and felt his way through the bushes. When he reached the quarry he groaned with relief before darting down the track to the Welshman's house. He almost broke the skin across his knuckles pounding on the door. Three heads popped out of a window above him.

"Who's doing all that banging?" cried an old man. "What do you want?"

"Let me in and I'll tell you everything," called Huck.

"Who are you?" said another voice.

"Huckleberry Finn. Now let me in."

"That's not a name that opens many doors," laughed one of the men. "But let him in, lads, and let's see what he wants."

Huck slipped through the gap as the door opened and almost ran into the old Welshman. The man's two sons stood watching from the stairs.

"Don't say it was me that told you," panted Huck.

"He'll kill me, for sure. But the Widow's been friendly to me over the years and I want to help her. But please, don't say it was me."

"Boys, he's shaking so much I reckon he *has* got something to tell," exclaimed the old man. "Your secret's safe with us, Huck. We won't ever tell."

A minute later the old man and his sons were climbing the hill, cradling shotguns in their arms. Huck went with them, as far as the path through the woods, and then hid behind a boulder. The silence rang in his ears until a shot split the night and he heard a scream. Huck didn't wait to hear any more. He sprang into the dark and sped down the hill as fast as his legs would carry him.

It was dawn before Huck dared to return to the Welshman's door. He rapped gently on the boards and a voice called: "Who's there?"

"It's only Huck Finn."

"That name can open my door day or night," replied the voice, warmly. "And welcome to you."

Huck thought these were the sweetest words he'd ever heard in his life. He was more used to receiving insults and disapproving frowns when he approached grown-ups around town. The door swung open and Huck saw the Welshman and his sons beckoning him to come inside.

"Boy, I hope you're good and hungry," smiled the Welshman. "Breakfast will be ready in a minute, piping hot and plenty of it. We were hoping you'd come and stay with us last night."

"I was scared," admitted Huck. "I tore off when I heard the shots and I didn't stop running until I reached the river. I've only come now because I was too curious to sleep. I need to know what happened."

"You do look pretty rough," said the Welshman. "But there's a bed here for you when you finish your breakfast. As for those devils in the woods, I'm sorry to say they got away. You took us to the right place and we were ready to pounce. But, at the last second I had a powerful urge to sneeze. There was nothing I could do to stop it. They heard the noise and took off into the woods, with us chasing and shooting after them. We lost them in the dark and ran into town to rouse the Sheriff. He got a posse of men together and went off to guard the riverfront. At first light, they're going to start beating their way through the woods, to try to locate the villains. We'll go down to help them as soon as we've eaten our breakfast. I wish we had a description of those rascals, Huck, but I'm guessing it must have been too dark for you to get a look at them."

"No, I saw them," replied Huck. "I followed them from town."

"That's splendid," cried the Welshman, clapping his hands in delight. "Describe them, boy."

"One's that old, deaf and dumb Spaniard that's been staying in town. The other's small and mean-looking."

"I know the men," declared the Welshman. "We saw them in the same part of the woods a week ago, casing the Widow's house. They slunk away when they spotted us. Boys, run down to the Sheriff with the news."

Huck jumped towards the door, putting a hand out to stop the Welshman's sons.

"Don't say it was me that told you about them," he pleaded. "I want to stay out of it."

"But you should get a reward for what you've done, Huck," answered one of the boys.

"My boys won't tell," interrupted the Welshman. "Your secret's safe, Huck Finn. Never fear."

The old man ordered his sons away and then asked Huck to sit with him at the table.

"We'll eat together," he said kindly. "But tell me first, why were you following those two villains?"

Huck thought carefully before he answered. "I couldn't sleep," he began. "When I'm restless, I like to walk and clear my head, so I took a stroll through the town. I saw two men leaving the tavern and it looked as though they were carrying something. It was so late, and they were so quiet, I was sure that they'd stolen something. When one of them stopped to light a cigar I got a look at their faces."

"You could see *both* their faces, from a single match?" asked the Welshman.

"I wasn't far away from them," replied Huck, struggling to get his story right. "I was suspicious, so I tracked them into the woods. That's where I heard the Spaniard say he was going to force his way into the Widow's house and hurt her."

"But you said that man was deaf and dumb," cried the Welshman.

Huck cursed himself for the mistake. He didn't

want the Welshman to guess the Spaniard's true identity, but his tongue seemed determined to get him into trouble.

"You have to trust me, Huck," said the Welshman. "Trust me, and I'll protect you from any harm. Now, tell me what you know about this Spaniard. It's obvious that you're hiding something. Trust me and I won't betray you."

Huck looked into the old man's honest eyes for a moment and then whispered in his ear: "He's not a Spaniard. He's Injun Joe."

The Welshman jumped up from his chair and slapped a hand down on the table. "I should have guessed it," he shouted. "When I saw him creeping around in the woods I thought there was something familiar about him. I should have caught him then. He's too crafty to be trapped by any posse, and he hasn't left any clues behind as to where he might be hiding. All we found last night was an old box."

"A box?" gasped Huck, thinking of the gold. "What was inside it?"

The Welshman waited for five, agonizing seconds before he answered: "Burglar's tools, of course. What's the matter with you boy? You look as if you've seen a ghost. What were you expecting to find in that box?"

"I don't know," stammered Huck. He was in trouble again, but it was good to know that the gold must still be in the tavern. Injun Joe wouldn't dare go back into town, so he and Tom could collect the treasure later. "If you remember, sir," Huck mumbled, "I thought they might have stolen something valuable in the town."

The Welshman chuckled. "I reckon they *were* planning to put something valuable inside it before the end of the night. But, thanks to you, we stopped them. Now let's eat."

Huck was still chomping on his breakfast feast when a knock at the door sent him running for a hiding place. The Welshman kept his promise and waited for Huck to hide behind some boxes on the stairs before he invited several men and women into the room. Huck recognized the Widow Douglas from her voice.

"I owe you a great debt of thanks," she told the Welshman. "You saved my life."

"You don't need to thank me, madam," replied the old man, blushing. "It was someone else that saved you, but he won't allow me to mention his name."

For ten minutes the Widow and her friends quizzed the Welshman about the mystery hero, but he wouldn't satisfy their curiosity.

"I'm sworn to silence and can say no more," he told the Widow, flatly. "But you owe your life to his bravery."

The story of the Cardiff Hill adventure spread quickly around town. It was a Sunday, and while the church congregation was still milling in the aisles, news came that the two villains had vanished from the woods. Judge Thatcher's wife hurried over to share this information with Mrs. Harper.

"That murderer's escaped," she sighed. "But the Widow's safe. And to think that my Becky's fast asleep in your house, missing all the commotion."

"But your Becky's not at my house," replied Mrs. Harper.

"Didn't she stay with you last night?" asked Mrs. Thatcher, startled.

"I'm afraid not."

Mrs. Thatcher turned pale and sank into a pew. She didn't notice Aunt Polly stepping over.

"Good morning, ladies," Aunt Polly declared. "I've got a missing boy to report. He's too scared or lazy to come to church, I imagine. Did Tom stay with either of you last night, by any chance?"

Mrs. Thatcher shook her head weakly and let out a sob. "They're both missing," she cried. "Let's call the children from the picnic together."

A moment later, the anxious parents were questioning a noisy crowd of children. None of the boys and girls could remember seeing Tom or Becky on the ferryboat. When one young man blurted out what everyone was thinking – that the pair must be lost in the cave – Mrs. Thatcher swooned to the ground and Aunt Polly burst into tears.

In less than five minutes, every bell in the town was ringing the alarm. Two hundred men set out to search the cave, including the old Welshman. He returned home early the next morning, spattered with candle wax, smeared with clay and worn out after walking miles through the labyrinth. The searchers had found nothing.

Huck was stretched out on a bed, delirious with a fever that had come on after his sleepless night in the woods. The Welshman sent for a doctor but every medic was over at the cave. The Widow Douglas heard about the sick boy not far from her house and offered to nurse him.

"I know some people say he's wicked," she told the Welshman, "but he's one of God's children. I'll do my best for him."

"He's not all bad," replied the Welshman, softly.

At noon, a group of exhausted men staggered into town. They had explored a thousand corners and crevices in the cave, firing pistols and shouting as they searched, but the children were still missing. One man had found the names *Tom and Becky* written on the cave wall in black smoke. Dozens of men had quickly trawled the alleyways around these markings, but the children must have wandered far away from the spot. They were walking the wrong way, heading deeper into the cold earth.

In the Caverns

When the other children in the cave had started their games of hide-and-seek, Tom and Becky had drifted away from them down a long tunnel. They were following the candle smoke writings on the low roof of the alleyway, made by thousands of previous visitors. Tom read out the jokes, sayings and signatures to Becky, until she suggested that they leave their own names on the rock wall. They dashed along the tunnel, looking for a bare patch of stone. In their hurry, they didn't notice the twists and turns they were taking, or that they could no longer hear the cries and shouts of their friends.

"Here's a fresh page for us," cried Tom, pointing up at an overhanging ledge.

Beck lifted her candle and wrote their names.

"Look over here!" called Tom. "There's a stream."

He dropped down a few steps into a new alleyway, holding his candle for Becky to see a trickle of sparkling water.

"There are more steps," said Tom, looking behind him. "It's almost like a staircase."

"Let's be explorers," giggled Becky. "We'll make a smoke mark on the wall to show us the way out."

They clambered down the steps, laughing and chatting as they moved into the secret depths of the cave. At one turn, they discovered a spacious cavern, with hundreds of thick stalactites hanging from its high ceiling.

"What's that black lump up there?" asked Becky.

Tom glanced up and saw a vast knot of thousands of bats nestled on the roof of the room. As he watched, the creatures burst into a cloud of flapping wings, squeaking and darting at the candles. Tom took Becky's hand and led her quickly into a side tunnel. With the bats chasing after them, the children ran down the alleyway, turning into another enormous, stone room.

"They don't like the candlelight," panted Tom. "But I think they've gone now."

"That's enough exploring for me," sighed Becky. "We'd better start back. Can you lead the way, Tom? It's all mixed up and crooked in my mind now."

"We can't go through the bat cave. We'll have to try another route."

"Those bats were horrible," agreed Becky, with a shudder. "But be careful, Tom. We don't want to get lost down here."

They started down a long corridor, walking in silence and peering into every turning.

"Oh, Tom," cried Becky, after ten minutes of fruitless searching. "They all look the same."

"Don't worry," he answered, trying to sound cheerful. "We'll find the way back soon."

"No," said Becky. "Let's go back through the bat cave. At least we know the way out from there."

Tom nodded and they turned around to retrace their steps. But, at the first branch of alleyways Tom hesitated. He couldn't remember if they had entered the tunnel from the left or right passage.

"Didn't you leave any marks?" squealed Becky.

"I was a fool not to," mumbled Tom. "I didn't think we'd be coming back again. I can't find the way, Becky."

"Then we're lost," she cried. "We'll never get out of this awful place."

Becky dropped to the ground, crying and wailing in despair. He sat down next to her, wrapping his arms around her and begging her not to give up hope. But it was only when he began to blame himself for the disaster that she lifted her face and wiped the tears away.

"It's not your fault, Tom," she told him, kindly. "You're no more to blame than I am."

They got to their feet and began shuffling along the stone alleyways, hoping to stumble across a familiar path. To preserve their light, Tom blew out Becky's candle and they advanced hand in hand, under the glow of a single flame.

The children had no way of telling the time, but after hours of moving through the caverns, Becky's legs refused to carry her any further.

"Can't we rest, Tom?" she pleaded.

"If we don't keep moving," he replied, "we'll never find the way out. But we can stop for a while, until you get your strength back."

They talked about their homes and families and how their friends must be looking for them. Becky cried and then closed her eyes to sleep. Tom sat watching her peaceful face until she woke and was ready to continue the search.

"We have to keep going," he told her. "Do you hear that dripping? I think there might be a stream ahead. Let's find it, and then we can rest again."

After a long search, they stumbled into a narrow alleyway and saw a small pool of water. Tom kneeled and took a sip.

"It's clean," he declared, and Becky joined him as he quenched his thirst.

"That's better," she said, wiping her lips. "Let's get moving again."

But Tom didn't get up from the floor. He propped the candle into a nook in the wall and turned to look at her.

"I have to tell you something," he said, earnestly. "But you must promise me that you'll be strong."

"I'll try, Tom," she replied. "But you're scaring me, talking like that."

"We have to stay here, Becky, where there's water to drink."

"Why, Tom?"

"Because that's our last candle," he whispered.

They watched their only source of light flickering and melting away before their eyes. At last, the flame spluttered and died and total darkness wrapped around them.

They talked in whispers, hugging each other for warmth and comfort. Tom promised that the cave must be full of searchers by now, and they could be rescued at any moment. But Becky had given up all hope of escaping the maze of underground passageways. She buried her face in Tom's chest, hiding her eyes from the dark.

"Hey!" snapped Tom, suddenly. "Did you hear that?"

Becky lifted her head and listened. She heard a faint, far-off shout. Tom answered with a yell and dragged her to her feet. They stumbled along the tunnel towards the sound of more shouts.

"They're coming," cried Tom. "Keep moving, but watch where you put your feet."

Almost trembling with joy and relief at the sound of the rescuers, Becky and Tom advanced slowly over the uneven rock floor. At a turn in the tunnel, Tom put his foot down and couldn't feel the path.

"There's a pit," he said. "I'll have to check it."

He kneeled and reached into the hole but his hand dangled in open space.

"I can't touch the bottom," cried Tom. "It could be a chasm, hundreds of feet deep. And there's no way around it."

"But the shouts are going away," sobbed Becky.

"It's no use," whispered Tom. "We can't get through this way. We'll have to go back to the pool."

The knowledge that there were people searching the cave nearby gave Tom renewed energy and hope. When he and Becky had taken another drink, he rummaged through his pockets.

"I've had an idea," he whispered. "I've got some kite string here. We can tie one end to a rock by the pool and start looking for a way around that chasm. The string will lead us back to the water."

Becky wanted to do anything but sit waiting in the darkness, and so she agreed to Tom's plan. A minute later the two friends were feeling their way along a turn in the tunnel, listening for any shouts in the distance. Tom was in the lead, leaning around a boulder that was blocking their way, when he saw a flicker in the darkness. He looked over and saw a human hand, holding a candle, emerging from behind a rock. Tom whooped with joy at the sight. But the next instant, a body followed the hand and Tom was paralyzed with fear. He was staring into the eyes of Injun Joe.

Tom's scream had startled the killer, and in the gloom of the cave he couldn't make out Tom's face. Injun Joe turned and ran, while Tom ordered Becky back to the pool.

"Why did you shout, Tom?" she asked him. "I couldn't see anything ahead of you."

"It was nothing," Tom lied. "I thought we should shout a few times in case anyone was nearby. But I'm thirsty again. Let's go back and rest."

"We need some food," sobbed Becky, as she followed the string to the water. "We can't survive if we don't eat. I don't think I'm strong enough to leave the pool again. Why don't you go out alone with the kite string, Tom?"

Tom thought of Injun Joe, hiding in the shadows.

"Come back and see me from time to time," added Becky. "I want you to be with me when my time comes."

"Don't say that, Becky," he yelled. "We're getting out of here alive."

"I can't see how," moaned Becky. "I'm so tired and hungry, I think I'll die here."

"Be strong, Becky," Tom pleaded. "I'll go looking again. There are lots of passages left to try. Hold on for a few more hours, and I promise I'll find a way out."

GOLD FEVER

By Tuesday afternoon, the town of St. Petersburg was in mourning for its lost children. Few people believed Tom or Becky would ever be found, and most of the cave searchers had abandoned the hunt and come home. Mrs. Thatcher was very ill and Aunt Polly's hair had turned snow white in her grief.

Long past midnight, the church bells began to peal. People rushed out into the road, shouting and waving lanterns. A lone rider thundered along the main street. "They've been found," he yelled. "The children are safe at the ferry landing."

The whole population of the town rushed towards the river to see Tom and Becky sitting in an open wagon, wrapped in blankets. A crowd swelled around the wagon and pulled it into town. Nobody went back to bed that night, and the townspeople had the greatest celebration anyone could remember.

At dawn, Tom was lying on a sofa, sipping hot drinks and entertaining an audience of excited friends with his story.

"I followed two tunnels as far as the kite string would reach," he explained. "But at the end of a third tunnel I saw a speck of light. I dropped the line and groped my way towards it. The light was coming from a tiny gap in a bank of earth and, when I squeezed my head and shoulders through the hole, I was staring at the Mississippi River rolling by. It was only by accident that I passed down that tunnel in the daytime. If it had been dark outside, we'd still be prisoners in the cave."

"You're a lucky boy," sobbed Aunt Polly, wiping her eyes and giving Tom a hug.

"It was a struggle to get Becky walking again," Tom continued, slipping out of his Aunt's arms. "She'd made up her mind that she was ready to die. But when she saw the light, she knew that we were free. I helped her to crawl out onto the grass and we lay there in the sun until some men in a boat spotted us. They thought I was spinning them a yarn at first, because we were *miles* from the entrance to the cave. But they rowed us to a house anyway. We rested for two hours and then they brought us to the ferry landing. And I've never been so happy to see St. Petersburg in all my life."

Tom and Becky were safe, but three days of hunger and cold in the cave were not easily shaken off. The children were weak and sickly after their ordeal. Tom was strong enough to walk a little on Friday morning, but Becky didn't leave her bedroom until Sunday, when she visited church with her mother.

Tom heard about Huck's illness on the Friday and rushed to the Welshman's house. But Huck was so weak, the Widow told Tom to come back in a few days. Even when he came back, she wouldn't leave Huck's side, and ordered Tom not to excite the patient with any wild stories about the cave.

People were still gossiping about the Cardiff Hill robbers and Tom heard every detail of the adventure from Aunt Polly. The smaller man's body had been discovered floating in the river and the Sheriff thought he'd drowned trying to evade his posse.

Almost two weeks had passed since the cave escape when Tom called in at Becky's house one morning. The Judge and some of his friends were drinking coffee in the kitchen. They started to joke with Tom about the cave.

"I bet you won't be going back there in a hurry," said one man.

"I'm not scared to go back in," Tom answered. "But I'd be more careful if I did."

"Nobody will get lost in that cave again," the Judge declared, firmly. "I've taken care of that."

"What do you mean, sir?" asked Tom.

"I ordered some of my men to put an iron door over the entrance two weeks ago," replied the Judge. "It's locked up tight and I've got the key."

Tom turned as white as a sheet.

"What's the matter, boy?" shouted the Judge. "Have you got something to tell me?"

"I have, sir," gasped Tom. "Injun Joe's inside the cave."

The Judge and the Sheriff gathered every able-bodied man in town and a dozen skiffs were soon bobbing across the river towards McDougal's cave. Tom was standing next to the Judge when he unlocked the cave. Injun Joe lay dead on the ground, with his bloodless face pressed up to the crack of light under the iron door. The killer's long knife lay next to him, with its blade broken in two from stabbing at the thick metal. Some marks on the rock showed where he had sucked moisture and drips from the cave wall. A few, torn bats were littered around the room. In his hunger, Injun Joe had eaten the animals, but he had still starved to death.

The Judge ordered the undertaker to bury the killer by the mouth of the cave. People flocked to his grave from miles around, drawn to the dreary place where Injun Joe had died, in the same way that they are often curious to see a public hanging. Tom pitied Injun Joe for the horrors he had suffered in the cave, but he wasn't sorry he was dead. For the first time in months, Tom's sleep that night was undisturbed by nightmares.

The morning after Injun Joe's funeral, Tom visited Huck and took him out for a walk in the woods. Huck soon told Tom that it was he who had warned the Welshman and saved the Widow.

"Why don't you tell her it was you?" suggested Tom. "You deserve all the credit."

"I'd rather keep my name out of it," replied Huck, crossly. "What if Injun Joe had some bandit friends, and they come looking for revenge? I'm more interested in the gold. Let's go back to the tavern tonight and collect it."

"But the gold isn't there," laughed Tom. "It's in the cave."

Huck's eyes blazed. "Are you sure?" he cried. "And do you know how to get to it?"

Tom nodded. "Will you go in there with me and help to get it out?"

"You try stopping me. When do we go?"

"Are you strong enough to set out for it now?"

"How far do we have to go in the cave?" asked Huck. "I've been walking around for a few days, but I'm not fighting fit."

"I know a path that leads straight to it," chuckled Tom. "I'll take you there in a skiff and I'll do all the poling."

"Let's go," whooped Huck.

"We'll need supplies," said Tom. "I don't want to take any risks in there. We'll take some bread and meat, some bags, two or three kite strings and lots of candles and matches. I don't want to run out of those again."

The boys gathered their things and found a skiff tied up above town. They left at noon, with Tom poling them towards woods on the opposite shore.

"Do you see that white mark above the trees?" Tom called. "There was a landslide on the hill over there. It's my secret marker. We have to land just below it."

They tied up the boat and pushed their way through some bushes.

"This is the best pirate hideout I've ever come across," laughed Tom. "Can you see where it is?"

Huck rummaged in the bushes but couldn't discover any opening or doorway. "There's nothing here," he grumbled.

Tom proudly marched over to a clump of bushes and dragged them back to reveal a small tunnel in the hill.

"I'm forming a gang of robbers," bragged Tom. "After all, hideouts are no use without a gang to hide things."

"Can I join?" begged Huck.

"You're the first one I was going to ask," answered Tom. "I thought Joe Harper and Ben Rogers might want to enlist with you."

"But who are we going to rob?"

"Anyone we come across," explained Tom. "We can keep them in the cave until they pay us a ransom. We'll be rich."

"It sounds better than being a pirate."

"It's much better. And we don't have to run away to an island. Let's go inside."

Tom led Huck along the tunnel until they reached the rock cavern where he had been trapped with Becky.

"It makes me shiver being here again," he whispered. "I'm glad you're standing next to me, Huck."

He guided Huck along the passage to where he had seen Injun Joe.

"Take a look at that big rock, Huck. Do you see anything written on it?"

Huck leaned into the cavern. "There's a *cross* marked there in smoke," he gasped.

"Do you remember what Injun Joe said, back at the haunted house? He talked about his den under the cross."

"I remember," replied Huck, in an amazed whisper. "This must be it."

"That's what I saw when I ran into him in the cave," said Tom. "Let's climb down there and hunt for the treasure."

They searched around the base of the rock but all they found were some old blankets, candle ends and chicken bones.

"Is that clay under our feet?" asked Tom, suddenly.

"I believe it is," said Huck, kicking the ground.

"Perhaps it really is *under* the cross," muttered Tom. "Let's dig."

He picked at the clay floor of the cavern and the blade of his pocketknife hit something hard.

"It's wood, I think," cried Tom. "It must be the treasure box – I always knew we'd get it!"

He pried the lid open with the blade and hundreds of gold coins scattered to the floor.

"We're rich, Tom, we're rich!" cried Huck.

"We'll pack it in the bags and haul it out," Tom shouted. "I'll be glad to get away from here. We don't want to run into Injun Joe's ghost, do we?"

Safely back at the skiff, the boys munched on a snack and lay in the sun chatting before they pushed away from the shore.

"We'll stash the money in the Widow's woodshed," Tom decided. "I'll come up in the morning and we'll count it and divide it."

They landed above town and started trekking up Cardiff Hill. When they reached the Welshman's house the old man came out to greet them.

"Come along with me, boys," he told them. "You're keeping everybody waiting."

"Where are we going?" asked Tom, keeping a watchful eye on the bags around Huck's shoulders.

"The Widow wants to see you," replied the Welshman, chuckling.

He herded them up the grand driveway to the Widow's house and Tom saw a crowd of people waiting on the steps.

"Half the town's here," said Huck, nervously.

Aunt Polly, Sid and Mary were standing in the throng. Tom's Aunt blushed when she saw the clay and mud stains on Tom's clothes.

"How do you get so filthy," she scolded, as the Widow stepped over to greet the boys.

"Come with me," she ordered. "We've been looking all over town for you. I've got some new clothes laid out for you upstairs, so you can clean yourselves up before the party starts. I'll leave you alone while you dress."

The moment the widow left the room, Huck dropped the money bags and ran across to a window.

"Let's find a rope," he whispered. "We can scramble down the wall."

"Why do you want go scrambling anywhere?" asked Tom.

"I can't stand crowds," snapped Huck. "And *fancy* crowds are the worst. I get edgy around high society and all the fancy people from town are downstairs."

"I'll take care of you," laughed Tom.

Sid appeared in the doorway. "We're waiting for you," he called. "You had us all worried again, Tom, going off like that."

"You don't need to worry about Sawyer and his gang," joked Tom. "What's the party for, anyway?"

"The Widow wants to thank the Welshman and his sons," explained Sid. "And the Welshman says he's got to get a secret off his chest. Now will you hurry up? We're sitting down for dinner."

It was a lavish meal but Huck was scratching at his collar and restless all the way through it. The Welshman finally got to his feet and called for silence. He told the whole story of Huck's bravery, adding that he thought Huck was too modest for his own good. If Huck had been ill at ease before this speech, it was nothing compared to his discomfort when it was completed. The Widow embraced him and invited him to come and live in her house. Huck stared down at the floor, crimson with his embarrassment.

"I'll pay for your education," she continued, "and when you're older I'll help set you up in business."

"Huck's rich already," interrupted Tom. He had spotted the opportunity for another of his dazzling schemes. "Huck's got lots of money," he continued, as the crowd began to titter. "And I can prove it to you."

Sid and the other children in the room were giggling as Tom ran upstairs. The giggling stopped when Tom returned carrying the heavy bags. He emptied the coins onto the dinner table, spilling them in every direction.

"Half of this treasure belongs to Huck," shouted Tom.

The adults circled around the table, gazing in silence at the pile of gold coins.

"Isn't somebody going to count it?" asked Tom.

The Welshman stepped forward and picked up a coin. "I'll do it," he declared.

He counted out twelve-thousand dollars into the sacks – more money than anyone there had seen in their entire lives.

BACK IN THE GANG

The Widow Douglas invested Huck's share of the money and Judge Thatcher did the same with Tom's, at Aunt Polly's request. The boys were suddenly wealthy and famous, but Huck had mixed feelings about entering *high society* and living at the Widow's house. After three weeks of torment in starched suits, soft beds and hot baths, he went missing. Tom tracked him down to an old barrel by the tannery. He was back in his old rags and smoking a pipe.

"You have to go home to the Widow's," Tom told him, abruptly. "She's worried about you."

"It doesn't work living there," Huck protested, grumpily. "I'm just not cut out for staying indoors and wearing fancy clothes. I like the Widow, but I can't stand all the scrubbing and the soap, and eating with a knife and fork, and wearing shoes. I just can't stand it. Being rich isn't what it's cracked up to be, Tom. It's all worrying and sweating and hard work. You can have my share of the money and leave me this barrel."

"You might get to like living in a house," Tom tried.

Huck spat. "I like the woods and the river too much. I wish we'd never found the money and we could go back to our plan of being robbers in the cave."

"You know, Huck," said Tom craftily, "all the best robbers are rich. There's no better disguise, because who suspects a rich man of being an outlaw. I'm starting the gang, but you have to be *high society* if you want to join."

"Don't throw me out," Huck pleaded. "I'll go back to the Widow's for a month, and see if I can find a way to bear it – if you'll let me stay."

"That sounds fair," smiled Tom. "We'll have our first gang meeting tonight, at midnight."

"I can't wait, Tom," cried Huck. "I'll stick to the Widow like glue if I can stay in your gang. And when I get to be a famous robber, she'll be proud of me."

"I reckon she will," chuckled Tom. "Proud as can be."

About Mark Twain

Mark Twain's best books are based around events from his own adventurous life witnessing the birth of modern America. Even his name is borrowed from one of his early romantic ambitions and a disappearing American symbol: the paddle steamer.

Twain was born Samuel Clemens, in 1835, and as a young man he trained to be a steamboat pilot on one of the country's great trading arteries, the Mississippi River. Deck hands measured the river's depth with a weighted line and shouted "Mark Twain" to inform the pilot that there were two fathoms of clear water below the boat. Clemens always liked wordplay and literary jokes, and when he started writing for newspapers he used this old river expression as his pen name.

He grew up in the state of Missouri, living in a remote frontier town called Hannibal. Surrounded by thick forests and the untamed wilderness, the townsfolk relied on the Mississippi for transportation and commerce. Clemens' family owned several slaves and he was raised in a culture that supported the horrors of slavery. In his famous book, *Adventures of Huckleberry Finn* (1884), he writes about a runaway slave called Jim. Critics claim that the writer could have said more in the story to condemn slavery, but his supporters argue that Huck's decision to help Jim shows that Clemens believed everyone deserved the right to be free.

Life was hard in the frontier country. Clemens was one of seven children, but three of his siblings died before he was seven years old. Pneumonia killed his father when Clemens was only eleven, and the young boy had to leave school and find work to help support his relatives. He set the metal type in place at a local newspaper office – his first brush with the publishing business.

After trying his hand at various occupations, Clemens trained to be a river pilot until the outbreak of war in 1861 stopped civilian river traffic. He fled west to escape the fighting, visiting the rough mining camps, trading posts and boom towns of Nevada and California. By 1865, Clemens was selling articles about his frontier exploits to local newspapers, signing them Mark Twain. He had a flair for comic anecdotes and storytelling and readers liked his witty observations and down-to-earth style.

In 1869 Clemens published his first book of travel pieces, *The Innocents Abroad*. It sold well and Clemens was soon established as a popular writer. He married into a wealthy family and settled in Connecticut to write the novels that made him one of America's most famous authors. His Mississippi stories, including *The Adventures of Tom Sawyer* (1876) offer a nostalgic vision of America before the sweeping changes of civil war and industrialization turned the country into a superpower. But Mark Twain also wrote tales about modern America and criticized politicians at home and abroad for their aggressive empire building in the years leading up to the First World War.

The last two decades of Clemens' life were rocked by family tragedy and financial problems, but he continued to write despite these setbacks. One of the crowning achievements of his career came in 1907, when Oxford University awarded him a special degree in literature. Clemens had come a long way since his barefoot wanderings along the Mississippi. He died of heart problems in April, 1910.